An Experiment in Navigation

Also by Rupert M. Loydell

Poetry
Ex Catalogue (Shadow Train 2006)
The Smallest Deaths (Bluechrome, 2006)
A Conference of Voices (Shearsman Books, 2004)
Familiar Territory (Bluechrome, 2004)
The Museum of Light (Arc Publications, 2003)
Home All Along (Chrysalis Poetry, 1999)

Prose
Stone Angels: Prose 1979-1993 (Magwood/Stride, 1995)

Collaborations
Risk Assessment [with Robert Sheppard] (Damaged Goods, 2006)
Make Poetry History [with Luke Kennard] (Miraculous Breath Books, 2006)
Shaker Room [with Lee Harwood] (Transignum, 2005)
Snowshoes Across the Clouds [with Robert Garlitz] (Stride, 2004)
Eight Excursions [with David Kennedy] (The Cherry On The Top Press, 2003)
The Temperature of Recall [with Sheila E. Murphy] (Trombone Press, 2002)
A Hawk into Everywhere [with Roselle Angwin] (Stride, 2001)

Rupert M. Loydell

An Experiment in Navigation

Shearsman Books
Exeter

Published in the United Kingdom in 2008 by
Shearsman Books Ltd
58 Velwell Road
Exeter EX4 4LD

www.shearsman.com

ISBN 978-1-905700-94-3

Copyright © Rupert M Loydell, 2008.

Cover painting, *Busy*, copyright © Rupert Loydell, 2008.

The right of Rupert M. Loydell to be identified as the author of this work has been asserted by him in accordance with the Copyrights, Designs and Patents Act of 1988. All rights reserved. No part of this publication may be reproduced, stored in a retrieval system, transmitted in any form or by any means, electronic, mechanical, photocopying, recording or otherwise, without the prior permission of the publisher.

Acknowledgements:
These poems, occasionally in earlier versions, first appeared in *Acumen, Aesthetica, The Argotist, Avocado, Borrowing a Voice* (Sherborne School), *Coffee House, Communique, Dusie, Eight Excursions* (The Cherry on the Top Press), *erbacce, The Eternal Anthology vol. VII* (Raunchland), *The Exeter Flying Post, Exultations & Difficulties, Eye, Flat Four, Great Works, Haiku Quarterly, Hummingbird, Intercapillary Space, Iota, Ixion, Jacket, Kindred Spirit,* Larry Norman's *Phanzine, Libertine, Liminal Pleasures, Litter, Maquette, Moodswing, Neon Highway, Only Connect* (Cinnamon Press), *Orbis, The Other Journal, Pages, The Poetry Cure* (Bloodaxe Books), *Poetry Kite, Poetry Provider* (Canongate), *Poetry Salzburg Review, Poetry Scotland, Popularity Contest, RLF Forum, Salzburg Review, Shadowtrain, Shearsman,* Robert Lax: *Speaking into Silence* (Stride Publications), *Stride, Tears in the Fence, Terrible Work, Third Way, The Matthews House Project, Wandering Dog, The Wayfarer, With.*

'A Fire in the House of Ice' was first published by Snowblind Books. 'Endlessly Divisible' was first published by Driftwood Publications. 'Secret Lifes' was first published by Skylight Editions.

Thanks to Clark Allison, Andy Brown, Peter Dent, Tony Frazer, Bob Garlitz, Major Gruntfuttock, Luke Kennard, Brian Pearce, Colonel Quaziborski, Jane Routh, Robert Sheppard, Martin Stannard, Sandra Tappenden, Alan West, my students and colleagues at University College Falmouth, and all our new friends in the village.

Contents

A Poem's Not For People	11

A More Personal Invention

White-Out	16
A More Personal Invention	17
Best to Be	18
The Lights are on at this Point	19
The Scheme of Things	20
The Poem I Do Not Want to Read	21
Talking to Myself	23
Crumbs	24
Fire	25
Clear Cut	26
Windfall	27
The Singing Time	28
Winging It	29
Not Like This	30
On the Horizon	31
Superhero	32
Unseen	33
The Man We Wanted God to Be	34
Cold Comfort	35
A Beautiful Wind	36
Taking the Life Out of Death	38
The Places He Did Not Know	39
Yesterday's Song	40
Thunder at the David Lynch Hotel	41
Hysterics	42
Nyctalopia	43
An Experiment in Navigation	44

Endlessly Divisible

A Characteristic Configuration	46
Asking for Directions	47
Convalescence	48
Creating a Context	49
Endlessly Divisible	50

Flesh and Fluids	52
Forty Minutes in the Magnetron	53
Invocations and Ritual Excursions	54
Journey of the Sun Boat	55
Long Shadows on a Dull Road	56
Maximum Overhang	57
Minimal Gesture	58
No Formal Inner Language	59
Overflow	60
Somewhere Soft to Land	61
Tangled Interchange	62
The Perfect Research Facility	63
The Stranger in Our Midst	64

The Uncertain Future

Acoustic Communion	66
By Heck	67
Characters from the Past	68
Defined by Opposition	69
Everyone Else	70
Food Chain	71
Glitter as an Effect of Sight & Sound	72
Hell, a Beginner's Guide to	73
Investigate the Process	74
January Morning	75
Know That	76
Languishing in a Motel	77
Mournful Delay	78
Not the Original Ending	79
Open Studio	80
Paintstripper	81
Questions will be Asked	82
Rock & Roll Singer	83
Self Portrait with Bottle & Bricks	84
The Geography of Escape	85
Under the Noses of the Powerful	86
Vanishing Point	87
Writing to an Audience	88
Xoanon	89

Youngster   90
Zealous   91

Spray Painting in the Dark
Crease Patterns   94
Arizona Sister Butterfly   96
Jazz Heart Electric   97
Paper Securities   98
Only One Animal was on My Mind   99
Full Given Name is Set Forth   100

Secret Lifes
The Secret Life of Anger   102
The Secret Life of Books   102
The Secret Life of Children   103
The Secret Life of the Creek   103
The Secret Life of the Dead   104
The Secret Life of Despair   104
The Secret Life of My Father   105
The Secret Life of the Igloo   105
The Secret Life of the Kayak   106
The Secret Life of Light   106
The Secret Life of Mist   107
The Secret Life of Music   107
The Secret Life of the Plumber   108
The Secret Life of Polemic   108
The Secret Life of Rain   109
The Secret Life of the Sky   109
The Secret Life of the Skylight   110
The Secret Life of Thunder   110
The Secret Life of the Treehouse   111
The Secret Life of the Village   111

A Fire in the House of Ice
Lines on the Point of Disappearing   114
A Fire In The House of Ice   118
Child's Play   120
Birthday   122
Double Act   123

Download	124
Igloo, Do We Go Around Houses	125
Igloo (i.m. Robert Lax)	126
Monochrome	127
Ad Reinhardt at the North Pole	128
This Appendix	129
Pre-Fab	130
Selected Evidence	131
The Me And The Here And The Now	133

Flipping the Script

Angel Trap	138
Aroma Fatigue	139
At Home	140
Consider this My Accidental Suicide Note	141
Counterfeit Word Jar	142
Cross-Purposes	144
Dedicated to Compulsion	145
Discontinuity	146
Entangled	147
Flipping the Script	148
Hallucogenic Tourism	149
I Guess that's Why You Called it The Blues	150
Its Own Journey	152
Just One of an Ongoing Series	153
King for a Day	154
Magpie	156
Milk Monitor	157
Neo-Shaman	158
Quite the Adoring Hologram	159
Speed of Light	160
Sunflower	161
Treading Some Well-Worn Tracks	167
Wild Root	168
Sources	169

for Natasha, Jessica and Sue

Let's go. Let's gargle into song. Let's
clear our phlegm-clogged
fucked-up throats, let's stutter our
dumb way into what
comes next.
>   —Don McKay,
>   'Song, for the Song of the Chipping Sparrow'

Put the tips of your fingers
On a baby man;
Teach him to be beautiful.
To hell with power and hate and war.
>   —Kenneth Patchen, 'Instructions for Angels'

A Poem's Not For People

a poem's not for people
who are afraid the sun won't rise tomorrow
who can help themselves but choose not to
who think giving advice is beneath them
who know the what but not the why

a poem's not for people
who are in a hurry to get a job
who want to work from home
who want their entertainment predictable
who hope their hotel room comes with an internet connection

a poem's not for people
who are easily dissuaded or discouraged
who can't follow a running gag
who pick and choose which laws they obey
who need to have simple answers

a poem's not for people
who pay attention to television
who have merely expressed an interest
who are easily offended
who giggle every time they see naked breasts

a poem's not for people who have never contemplated Helen of Troy
and wondered at a face that could launch a thousand ships

a poem's not for people
with queasy stomachs
with memory loss
with no attention span
with plans for the future
with guns in their homes

a poem's not for people
who won't accept their responsibility to analyze and understand

a poem's not for people
who sleep too much
who don't have a social life
who don't know what they want to do
who want to make other people do the same things

a poem's not for people
with nothing better to do

a poem's not for people
who can provide visions to order
who want to know who they were in a past life
who simply want to avoid hell and gain heaven instead
who are looking for special effects and bombs bursting in the ear

a poem's not for people
who don't like subtitles or weirdness
who are tired of spending half their lives in gridlock
who can't have an intelligent conversation
who are a burden and a threat
who are just passing through
who never do anything wrong
who are trying to cooperate
who know there is more to give
who are afraid of the dark

a poem's not for people
who don't like bone-rattlingly loud music
who like their songs to clock in under seven minutes
who aren't in the orchestra
who have two left feet
who dabble in the field
who take such things seriously

a poem's not for people
who are used to seeing somebody die before their eyes
who are mindless drones locked up in an artificial reality
who cannot stand being crowded or uncomfortable
who can't abide the idea of someone sleeping in their bed
who want big families with lots of kids
who are thinking about doing some project but have not yet started it
who think they have everything right and need nothing else
who say they haven't the time to learn

a poem's not for people who can't find their way blindfold

A More Personal Invention

White-Out

Driving into the grey
with a truckload of worries
and the radio's dull presence,
morning gradually lightens;
wipers smooth the rain away.

I like it when I find me out of context:
the travel news cuts into the music
with a burst of conceited dissonance
one last time before the white-out.
Snow flurries and sleet sticks all over,

the world streaks past at light speed
and I am dizzier than ever, teased
to the point of tottering. How various
we are, looking beyond what is about us
to what might be out there, unseen.

A More Personal Invention

The poet's year of silence
is by its very nature
a medium of strangeness,

a fuguelike weaving of words
searching for radial innocence,
increased understanding of the world.

Best to Be

right at the edge of things, watching them fall apart.
Never arrive early, always leave before the end;
don't let people know your name or where you live.

Question the importance of attendance and make sure
it is understood you are there under sufferance. Say no
to requests for help and to questions of commitment.

Practice being unseen: shadows are to skulk in.
Always wear dark clothes and keep your distance.
Let people know you prefer to think about things,

not do them. It is more important to understand
than to experience, better to stamp on graves
than keep things alive. Your life has been hard.

Remind people of this loudly and often.

THE LIGHTS ARE ON AT THIS POINT
for Martin Duxbury-Hibbert

Another flickering cartoon day dawns,
which I now have to fill for two of us;
penguins and bears won't amuse for long.

On the island of dreams you will not be stirring yet,
though I call to you with memories of green paper
from ten years ago, when poems flew between us,

exchanged in a constant flutter and flurry of mail.
Time and energy then were endless; now, exhausted,
I read aloud in one-sided companionable dialogue.

Another writer bullies me in his dreams, exploring
underground expansions, possibilities he insists
include several volumes of his new work. I decline

to indulge him. We pan out to view the author's photo,
circa 1965, where he and his father look just the same.
This is disturbing, though salutory for our narcissism.

Difference and shadow, pieces of paper for amusement.
Small books and mail art, a pair of UFO sunglasses;
best wishes from the man. I wonder how you are?

The Scheme of Things
Italy, July 2006

This is just a pause, time out from stone steps
and a dungeon with no way out, to dial home.
There's decorating to be done and only a few weeks off.

Hands over our sunburnt ears, we hold reddened faces
up in surprise to wooden balconies. How to see everything?
It's the second time for me; at least the pressure's off.

I only hear the bell right above us, can't catch my breath
or balance the thrill of unknown destinations with art & history,
the comfort zone of going back up the castle tower.

We can see the smallest villages as sunset softens the mountains,
navigate where we've been before. How the animals sprawl and loll.
Let's drink Croatian beer and find a place to eat in the shade.

It's over 100° until late when we swim at the nearest bar. It's good
to know particular places and where to park, how to break my habits:
I haven't painted since before the move, places I've been to stay pictured.

Small lizards on the terrace, brown bears on broken concrete, wolves
pacing shadowy cages. Tiny tortoises hundreds of miles from home.
How do I know my way around this zoo? Folded pocket map.

The Poem I Do Not Want to Read
for David Grubb

This is the poem I do not want to read
but you asked me to. The one that
is more than language, that cuts
through the crap and makes me cry.
I hope you are proud of what you
have done, have made poetry do?
I prefer linguistic puzzles and games,
do not like to be upset or reminded
of what can be said or how to say it.

This is the poem I do not want to read.
It arrived in a book full of angels
and light, orchards and relatives,
ghosts from your past. The wars
you have been to revisited, along
with the madness you've seen.
I would rather not be told about
these things. How dare you
make words so meaningful.

This is the poem I do not want to read
but felt I ought to. Out of the marvellous,
toward epiphany, angels sing and words
are on fire, if you catch my meaning.
Or rather, if I catch *your* meaning, the
drift of where you are going. Where
are you going? The memory room is
no place to live – the past will fade,
the only view is next year's rain.

This is the poem I do not want to read.
Our church clock won't be wound up
ever again – it's electric, plugged in
to the mains. The orchard you remember
has been felled, they don't make cider
with apples any more. We all have our
individual methods for pushing away
what we don't want to know, and this
is mine. Silence may tell stories but

this is the poem I do not want to read,
the poem that saves me talking to myself
or others, that gets through nostalgia to
the heart. It is the poem that says *look,
I am here* and bathes in full moon's light.
But when clouds confuse the moment
and it is impossible to read in the dark,
I am forced to remember you speaking
this poem that I do not want to read.

Talking to Myself
for Sandra

I was listening to Sandra. She told me
she'd been yacking with James about how,
if she had dared to wear the wrong shoes,
she would have been beaten up at school.

I was talking to myself about self-discipline
and poems. Desire's giggling under the bed,
ambition is absent as expected. I wanted
to say something sensible about footwear

but have been reduced to focussing upon
the mechanisms of narrative. The connection
between shoes and story is an illusion,
a flame flickering over the poem's surface

as words snag and retard the assertive
motion of speech throughout our lives.
Even the ground under our feet
is beyond the narrator's control.

Think about things that burn and what
you can do with fire. It's all right to talk
to your friends as long as they are listening.
Only one thing remains inconstant: death.

I wrote to Martin about his father dying,
only managed a short, apologetic note.
There are no instructions to be followed
when finding substitutes for parents.

Think about where we are walking and
what might lie beneath: pain and suffering
trodden into the mud, joy sprinkled on
the grass like frost. Careful how you tread.

CRUMBS
for Brian

Today, I imagined you drinking tea
from a china cup and saucer, and
dropping crumbs on the brown jacket
you always wear. Peering uncertainly

at the world in a steamed-up café,
you were wondering how to capture
the past, which has yet to catch up
with itself in this small Dorset town.

In the abbey, someone wanted
to tell me all about the place,
wouldn't let the silence speak.
I smiled thinly and moved away.

Later, I saw you in the park, scarf
and overcoat on, pondering what
to write, wondering why the world
had changed and wouldn't let you be.

The past is attractive, but now the train
is taking me home. Even there, tomorrow
has yet to arrive. I dunk my biscuit
in memory and watch time drip away.

Fire

Fire's first inside you, a flicker of light,
a moment's passion, sudden heat or spirit sign:
sunflowers against summer blue, shooting stars piercing black.

The blazing camp fire, logs stacked high,
is cold petals, grey ash in your hair,
when you wake up in the morning.

Home's tame version is the same,
a hearthful of cinders and charcoal;
if you're lucky a red ember still shining.

Naming is losing. Fire's a flicker of light,
a moment's passion, sudden heat or spirit sign:
tongues of fire above the apostles' heads.

Through fire, through earth, through wind,
we know the world. Sit in the dark and hear
the world hum, watch the electrocuted sky

as fireworks burst and spray above,
explosions of scribbled colour. The night burns;
bonfires collapse, flame, flare and glow.

Naming is losing. Fire's first inside you,
a flicker of passion, sudden heat or spirit sign;
in partnership with water, earth and air.

Clear Cut

The days are already too full, she says,
and I know they don't get any emptier.
Her everything now is black and white
but for me nothing is clear cut or easy.

A wolf at the door asks me to vote for him.
I can think of no reason to do so. Labels
are usually meaningless, each day's a surprise;
things are almost always in their wrong place.

In a new anthology, my poem gasps for breath,
a fiction among true stories of disease and dying,
endless poems about how ill the author feels.
My voice has been borrowed; now her's scrapes

and stings with new-found truths, a steel blade
across mind's chin. My hope is that she will find
a kind of contentment I haven't found, be at ease
in a world where things are clear cut and easy.

Windfall
Jessica Rose

Singing as
you paused
halfway out,

bottom lip
quivering
in surprise,

mouth alive
with music,
you arrived:

a bruised plum
falling into
the world.

The Singing Time

Your world's still small
and full of cuddly toys
which share the singing
time before you sleep
and sunshine moments
when you first wake.
You know your own mind
and want things your way.
You don't know, just think
you can. Then do. I am
concerned about our future
because that is where we
are going to be tomorrow.
You ignore me when I call
and climb unguarded stairs
towards your room, sometimes
my study, where office chair
becomes a roundabout.
Experience is an open letter
you write home every day.
Tell me this isn't strange,
your life passing me by.

Winging It

Winging it. Always grabbing the time
and trying to fit things in to short days,
to finish books started a long time ago
or listen to music in any spare moments.

Memory adds further facts; the plot expands.
I am inclined towards doing something else
or doing nothing; have an inner demand to look.
Can no longer remember the way to come here.

A child's footsteps criss-cross each day;
a small voice cries in the night.
'Towards the end he lived
only in the province of himself.'

Not Like This

Could anyone kill their own child? She in mud and
realising it was first topic of my brain this morning,
we managed discussion in the classroom.

Once tucked up in bed,
my daughter sunburns away the haze,
prays for Mary and her mum.

School issues statement.
Everyone is talking about what's happened;
it doesn't involve themselves.

Could they have helped death or distress?
Is there anything to do as others have done?
Weak tea in the playground can't undo.

Suddenly I'm in a story where a body is found
and the killer sends a letter home.
Everyone wants to know, but confesses.

I would rather be finding out.

On the Horizon

The stranger has left, leaving the door open,
changing our notion of what is beautiful.

I see him still, absent without leave
in the middle of a heat wave; the very room.

My life is as difficult to structure
as a caress or handclasp, a lingering kiss.

I hunger for a taste still to be created,
the great blessings time can confer.

Superhero

When I heard about the explosions
this morning, I phoned my mum
to stop her travelling uptown,

then watched the news. Later,
a couple of people called and
some books came for review. It's late

but I can't sleep. Crowds pour out of
bombed stations onto London streets
full of sirens and lights, dayglo jackets

and red tape. I don't care what
the queen or prime minister think,
don't need to know whose fault it is,

I just want someone to save the world.

Unseen

I went to the pub for a drink, a shandy
because of the heat. I wanted to support
merit and diversity, to wonder and worry.
Have I got the right shoes on today?

Have I hell. *Fashion victim* is too polite
a term, I'm in the clothing wilderness,
especially when it rains. Damp trousers,
sodden shoes, a leaking leather jacket;

no-one takes a shine to it or me. There's
no reason anyone should, I'm too short
and it's far too early to be supping ale.
Time is an unusual enemy; the weather

doesn't help. Wet and warm, badly dressed
and stuck in our own ways, we each wear
our human face in the likeness of a god who
made the rain and visits cathedrals unseen.

THE MAN WE WANTED GOD TO BE
from a phrase by Peter Porter

The man we wanted God to be
is divorced and drinks on his own.
He watches too much television
and is never far from the settee.

The man we wanted God to be
has no motive or reason.
He doesn't turn up for interviews,
if he did wouldn't get the job.

The man we wanted God to be
can hardly find his own way home
or remember the way into town,
let alone manage to walk on water.

The man we wanted God to be
turned out to be somebody else.
His stories only confused us,
we didn't much like his friends.

The man we wanted God to be
is still insistent that he is.
We had such high hopes for him
but heaven was not on his mind.

Cold Comfort

'Who put the Bible in the fridge and does it matter'
—'Notes on a Work in Progress', David Grubb

Would it have been better in the oven? Or
in a drawer, perhaps Gideon's bedside drawer?
If love is red hot and God is love then maybe
the fridge is the best place. Someone simply
made a mistake, thought it was lasagne or
a bottle of milk. Both metaphors we could
tease out if you want: *The word of the Lord
came to me as fresh milk flowing, giving me
calcium to enrich my frail bones.* And we all
know a Mediterranean diet is best – so soak
that Bible in olive oil and eat it with a nice
green salad. Honestly, I don't understand
your concern. Inspired or not – apocryphal
or history, myth or story, idea or truth –
there are plenty more copies to be had.

Mind you, putting my teenage Bible in the bin
two weeks ago, I felt guilty. I couldn't stand
its slang, the way it tried so hard to be hip,
or the peeling dayglo stickers on the cover.
Was Jesus a surrealist? Might he have been
if he'd lived today, not then? Where on earth
would he keep his Bible? What would he make
of religion today? I dread to think. My sister's
a reverend now, but speaks of doubt and
her struggle for faith, which is reassuring
if perverse; I mean to commit to questioning
within the church. Anyway, we'd best chill out.
Keep your Bible somewhere safe and let your
work progress. Make sure the fridge door is
firmly shut, your power supply switched on.

A Beautiful Wind
Brian Louis Pearce, 1933-2006

Overhearing voices, attempting to name
strangeness, mixing texts and opening
memories, I desperately delay grief.

Vans were being loaded as I found out
that you had already dashed on ahead,
made your final ever move. Checkmate,

game ended, pieces tipped over in disarray.
If we could live with no sense of dying
we wouldn't be human, you wouldn't be you.

You are no longer you. Reaching beyond
sorrow I ponder this particular death,
your private navigation of the world.

Living in the house full of holes,
your imagination is given free reign,
room to manoeuvre and dart, outwit

the angels and confuse new neighbours
with oblique reference and obsessions,
playful puns, your perceptive talk.

The possibility of possessing happiness
seemed always pushed aside; words
were ever so much more important.

Now you will never answer my questions
nor compile that reader you planned.
Another unpublished novel of yours

is hidden in my computer's memory,
many more in your abandoned brain.
You might learn to let go of language,

experience drive you along, rather than
recall and capture. You might learn to
dance or fly, be given perfect sight.

You are in the house full of holes now,
where you always knew you would be.
It is a beautiful wind that blows

the spirit home. Having begun by
calling for truth we must now trust
the silence and question no more.

A beautiful wind blows wherever you are.

Taking the Life Out of Death

Holiday plans the future:
gated compound way down south,
warm home to retire to.

The barman explained
to the old folks at lunchtime
it was chips *or* mash, not both.

Music from long ago in the mail,
borrowed CDs and counterfeit copies
from strangers and new friends.

Easier to map out fictions
and wallow in distant sounds
than deal with linear time.

Someone on the phone,
twenty years after we last spoke,
sounds younger than he should.

Comfort zone, safe houses,
dim memories, bright lights:
the disturbing dynamics of dreams.

THE PLACES HE DID NOT KNOW
for Phil Bowen

He lives in exile
from imagined countries.
Hers was one of them.

    She said the present wasn't right.
    Love was something they'd never know.

He lives in exile
from a time that wasn't now;
a welcome home in the evening.

    She said the present wasn't right
    so he had to take it back.

He lives in exile
from a romance
that could have happened.

    She doesn't know or notice
    what he imagines.

He retraces his steps
erasing the years of
might-have been.

    She sounded good-looking
    on the phone.

Yesterday's Song

Winter is a colourful bird
who perches on the books
around my room. I absorb
words by osmosis and hope
her wings are stronger than
the makeshift shelves; sun
warmer than language as it
blossoms upon spring's page.

In the old magazines you
mailed me, I found a photo
of desire, dressed in fishnets
and more eyeliner than is
fashionable today. I forget
what she sang or where she
made her nest; wish I could live
wherever the music came from.

This poem begins where it should
end as yesterday's song flies away.

Thunder at the David Lynch Motel
for Martyn and Steve, rather late

We are deconstructing the day
with a bottle of bourbon to hand;
three upright chairs moved
to the balcony outside our room:
best place to see the storm's display.

Naked in a bath of electricity,
we absorb sheet lightning
falling down the distant stars;
our own memories of America
a library of quirks and contrasts.

Widescreen effervescence
delays departing afterburn,
a retinal image of the unknown:
horizon bigger than we've ever seen
above the empty swimming pool.

Hysterics

'We were there much longer
than you recall', you said.
I remembered that today.
And also the sunshine in
Manhattan, and the smell
of pine when the plane
stopped to refuel in Canada,
twenty years ago. These
moments linger, jostle
with words and music.

So many places I'll never
see again; so many places
you may never see at all.
Already we've crowded
your life with choices;
too many – you're confused.
I can see it in your eyes,
choosing what to do next,
wondering what to value
most; guessing our response.

New and uncertain configurations;
life is thoroughly compelling.
I don't know whether to
worry and debate, or just be
happy to find interest and
an unusual mind at work.
Around me fathers and friends
are dying, and you have hysterics
about the beached dolphins
who aren't even in this poem.

Nyctalopia

The house of birth is a complete unknown,
something we possess but can't remember.
No words, no voice, only breath & scream;
problem pictures with no knowledge.

We'll never own what our mother knew
nor learn to see in the light of day.
I am happiest in the dark or dusk;
the image in my head has come to stay.

Well, here we are again, swamped with
the slow draining numbness of winter flu.
Time to consider the war and our reasons;
we will soon be running out of world.

Certainty is a wonderful gift,
one I don't happen to own.
May democracy return to haunt
those always sure of what's right.

An Experiment in Navigation

Mixed media thought engines,
instruments of communication and comprehension,
lost in the anonymous noisy jumble of landfill.

A chain reaction of references and suggestions
losing its wish to be useful;
an elementary lack of balance and impulse control.

The echo of the original becomes ever fainter:
weird skanks, cosmic abstractions and fake folk pieces,
fiery snakes, red skies and golden beings…

I have no idea how to decipher this map

Endlessly Divisible

A Characteristic Configuration

The growth of human knowledge
can be moulded into different shapes,
information and movement fitted
into maps, diagrams and tables.

The proof of this is similar
to what we saw earlier today:
ideas moving with enormous speed
from one side of the mountain to the other.

Nothing is ever destroyed in combustion,
matter is simply transformed.
Oil and air turn into living substance
which we breathe in whenever we inhale.

In a world where actuality is spacious,
and prospects outshine the real,
poetic form remains obscure,
continental drift the same.

At closing time, or after,
we'll experiment for hours,
try and disturb the imagination;
experience helps us to grow.

Truth lives just over the horizon.

Asking for Directions

Allowing puddles to shine
involves an ability to discard
unease and primitive desire.

It is obvious that light
is an outdated metaphor
expressing a desire for God.

He's *supposed* to be there,
dangling in the moment,
overseeing the eternal.

What does holiness obscure?
The full and final take. So what?
The tape stops then restarts again,

catches one last moment of invention:
our attempt to divide the atom
and find the breaking point.

The book is never opened.

Convalescence

I have a new vocation as a hostage,
am trying to encourage strange encounters
but resources seem inadequate.

Floundering through inbetween,
asking for clearer directions,
time itself is in reverse.

Wouldn't it be strange if
we could remember the future
and decipher a portion of our lives?

We'd understand everything then:
transformation and perception,
the inscribed surface of the self.

Resistance is quizzical; the scratch
and flicker of belief turns out to be
only another exotic wonderland.

Admit it: we create the world
then allow it to contain us.
This is variable evolution:

dreams receding behind cardboard.

Creating a Context

Welcome to the house of cold, where the morning
is spent clearing the head, the nose and throat,
and the afternoon quietly resting and moaning
until the evening phlegm sets in. In the town
where I'm now working, Sion is half way up the hill.

Learning's at the top, though most of it is now
a giant building site inside a blue wood fence.
Banging doors and radiators, we wander around
trying to find the enemy. I will not be fooled by time:
tense is never perfect, and very rarely present;

the past tends to intervene. Faith makes it impossible
for us to speak of God in the same breath as enigma,
almost necessary for us to cross the line on which this
argument depends. I must stop refusing to be brilliant,
dispense with using words. I will stay in the shower

until I rust. Someone has to do this at some point,
the resulting archive will be a fascinating insight.
My life was conceived as a number of feedback loops,
distorted sounds, with dreams and doubts ignored.
The kind of music of which you'd no doubt disapprove.

I can almost hear you in another story, moving
from chapter to chapter. When you came back
everything was different, but you seemed
mentally prepared for change. However,
I still can't find the eternal resting place.

Through the plane and into volume, sides and bottom
frame the void, with a neat roof made of felt and fat.
Confined to the space of this page in this book,
with only occasional visits to town, how can I know
if I'm inside or outside? Even, perhaps, over the fence.

Endlessly Divisible

Until I forget it again
I understand everything.
Thoughts thrown from the train
are piled up high by the rails:

a circle of embers and ash,
consistency slowly thickening,
as garbage does whenever
abandonded in the sun.

Is there something left?
Right here. It's writing.
Words run down my throat;
the show's just getting good.

You can see real well
from the plastic chair
placed on the kitchen roof
where sunlight sometime stays.

It's cheaper than a deck
and better than a yard.
As long as the ceiling holds,
what a glorious view it is:

same window, same café,
allotments left to weeds,
time and traffic passing by,
as colour fades away.

Limits are difficult, if not
impossible to establish.
What I just saw in the hall
was an attempt to share the guilt.

Moving from past to present
I surprise myself by getting lost.
Memory runs down my thought;
please wipe away past hurt.

Information is becoming lifelike:
choice after choice of imaginary delicacies.
I'm not the hardest chocolate in the box
but it's clear that time is space.

Sunlight detonates and explodes,
stars hammer into the sky.
Now that everyone is everywhere
compensation must be sought.

Flesh and Fluids

After forty minutes
in the magnetron
I wait for the world

to quieten around me,
for someone to offer
access to the miraculous.

Are there coffins
in the crypt? How long
does dying take?

I still intend
to climb the rock fall –
no-one can take my place.

This cancer is like
a loved-one held hostage
and never allowed to go.

Forty Minutes in the Magnetron

'Do you agree or disagree with the following statement:
it bothers me my life did not turn out as I expected.'
— 'Evolution', Jorie Graham

The earth is shaking. The hum
is not disguised by music
through the headphones, fear

is not disguised by my casual
demeanour. I am barely
decent in a hospital gown,

am a tree of flesh and fluids.
Uncertainties remain uncertain:
"Someone will be in touch soon."

Unspoken words are all too clear,
seem to be creating a context.
I'm curious to see what might happen.

Got a million excuses for doing nothing,
am going to waste time worrying about
the use of useless things that might not be.

Collage is a form of memory.
My new painting is called *painting*,
but this poem is not called 'poem'.

I sense the impulsive movement
of the future moment, seek
a much more secure image of myself

as I listen to the heating
creak its way toward morning.
I have been awake since 3am.

Invocations and Ritual Excursions

So, writes my seaside correspondent,
does dark matter swirl around in orbit?
Behind the mirror's another world
he reckons is no stranger than our own.

An orientation towards the visible,
a concentration of sense impression:
the objects he chooses declare
innumerable traces of the human.

Suggestions of personal injury remain:
sooty information on burnt glass,
stitched ochre shadow outlines,
a canvas with black letters at the top.

The archaeologist of paint
cuts back through long-dry layers
to the source of disrespect:
reflections in a moving window.

What's interesting is the urge to keep.
What stays or goes? Paper's piled high,
each scrawl and gesture, splash and spot,
saved then annotated for a *Complete Works*.

I took some poems to Mother Sarah
which I thought might be of use.
As token poet in the scientific midst
my presence is written only in chalk,

a discontinuous trace with no known
connection to the past. Pockmarked words
are a slight release. Perforated by
raw doubt and mainly made of matter

I find myself uncertain, circling belief.

Journey of the Sun Boat

The journey of the sun boat never begins.
It has been delayed by the sale of a house,
a joyrider crashing into our car
and the eternal problem of original sin.

Maybe we'll be blown all the way to heaven
and learn to look seagulls in the eye?
Turning the afterlife into an adventure
changes more than a person's resolution.

A hundred boots are laid out on the beach,
all looking for somewhere to walk to.
But I know I've already been there;
this playful voyage never stops.

Long Shadows on a Dull Road

The rest of the space is dark,
though if you focus
you can sense the possibilities
that surround us.

What you see is what you get:
there is nothing to unravel.
Death and life will never meet,
collision is not physically there.

The secret of a good life is this:
we share a common stem.
The secret of a good lie is this:
no-one can ever be sure.

Love is just another experiment
likely to end in failure,
an inert precious metal
with the imprint of the sacred.

Memory requires devotion.

Maximum Overhang

The imprint of the sacred entails an other.
From paint to neon, from neon to pixel,
everything in the landscape becomes information
oscillating between fusion and diffusion,
a slow-pace version of life
systematically pursuing an ideal
round and round a tangled interchange,
hindering the possibility of comprehension.

Minimal Gesture

Memory requires devotion.
The effect of this is remarkable:

a thin strand from ceiling to floor
and back up to the ceiling

brings the moon down.
Each and every time.

No Formal Inner Language

Awake since 3am,
I note death much in evidence:

meandering down the slope
like a rain-flushed stream.

I prefer not to get wet
in the middle of the day.

Give the viewer
a feeling of space:

connect with sorrow,
sympathise with age.

Electrical discharges
sputter along the margin,

colour wouldn't dare
to hang on to my easel.

Thought is ephemeral,
a site-specific installation.

The rest of the space is dark.

Overflow

Energy swirls in vocation: the train is again delayed,
these impromptu lakes seen much later than planned.
A different route today, same journey with another view.

Find the always in the breaking point, follow a thread
through to the wrong side of inbetween. We are dispensable:
morning finds us abandoned in evolution's snowy margins.

Archaeology cuts back through long-dry layers of self
to the source of disrespect: reflections in a moving window.
Everything in the landscape contains hidden information.

Something lives in the scratched and flickering suburbs,
spilling golden light across these empty fields and railway line.
The evening brings the moon down, starts to unravel time.

Somewhere Soft to Land

When you came back everything was different
and you seemed prepared for constant change.
What interested me was the urge to keep moving
through the beep and chime of everyday,
finding answers in the swirl of neon and pixel.

I tried to place you in another story, one where
life is conceived as a number of feedback loops
and distorted sounds, a number of feedback loops
and distorted sounds, infinite doubts and dreams;
endless memories, strong associations of self.

My life threads through itself, distorting time,
diffusing or ignoring all my dreams, desires.
Faith is a rain-flushed stream overflowing into doubt,
wish fulfilment is impossible: the future is still there.
Imagined possibilities are present in every question.

I prefer not to take fading pictures off the wall:
the visible is stranger than what we think we see.
Rituals are an attempt to share unacknowledged guilt;
the tape stops the skid, we are learning how to fall.
All I want is a thin head and the occasional word of praise.

Tangled Interchange

Memory requires devotion,
time itself can be reversed:
ghostly images of a former age.

Things are endlessly divisible in theory
but not in actual fact. Families are
preposterous yet stubbornly perplexing,

a thin strand connecting blood cells,
architectural and artistic features,
in understanding of shared past.

Mum whisks the carpet sweeper fast
and we run back to honeysuckle days
when we slept with the landing light on.

Empty our desks and take fading pictures
off the wall. If the right sort of camera
had been invented, we'd take photos of it all.

I'll be glad when this obsession is over,
and I can divorce this sharp sensation of pain.
Something is falling from the sky:

wish fulfilment, guilt, familiar sensations.

The Perfect Research Facility

The golden light is always in the next field
but the journey of the sun boat never begins.

Energy swirls in every direction,
detouring miles across the marshes;

distance stretched until it becomes
an invisible thread of influence.

We are homesick for the high street,
have picked the best spot with some care,

check mirrors when we can,
to see if our reflections are still there.

Time's current flows in two directions,
strong associations are released.

Angels live in the suburbs,
faith drives me to the station;

my application for messiah has been
turned down. No reason has been given.

I'm left with a handful of eggs
and a beard nobody much likes.

The Stranger in Our Midst

The eskimo in the net,
the elephant by the tower,
the entomologist at work:

imagined possibilities
present in our questions,
show the stranger's spirit.

Their eyes are usually brown,
nose most unusually broad.
Type of hair is unimportant.

Their way of life is simple,
with no time for the arts.
They hatch into tiny grubs.

Their rituals, which resist corrosion,
are most unpleasant to watch;
they have special music for the dance.

The formula for understanding this?
A pat on the head and a word of praise.
Truth is confirmed and established.

Table A is for precision jumping,
B shows the emission of gas.
Experience will help us to live:

whenever we breathe we inhale.

The Uncertain Future
(Risk Assessment 2)

'This poem never ends and tomorrow
is waiting to get its words in.'
 — David H.W. Grubb, 'This Poem Never Ends'

'Everything is surface and appearance.
To be is to be perceived.'
 — Steven Shapiro, *Connected*

'I like to satisfy the crowd with absences'
 — Peter Dent, 'Sort and Classify'

Acoustic Communion

what was once opaque   emotions   ideas   fears
does not fit in to what we know   pre-existing things
a dark shape in a dark room   says nothing I can hear
new concepts & theories   concrete   visceral   known

diary of thoughts & emotions   last chance sales-drive
the bondage of transient emotion   my favourite disease
painters of the lost paradise   beauty veiled by clouds
house that I once lived in   unexpected dome of day

puddled mud & polar lights   message on the ground
adults   drop-outs   inmates   people all around
mixed metaphors are dangerous   mind can leak away
the image speaks in silence   blinks across the sky

hymns & blues   parlour ballads   crash of pots & pans
between the borders of the world   dreams & visions   signs
flooded creeks & fallen angels   where are you going so soon?
the middle ground of happiness   the loneliest place of all

By Heck

general opportunities   find out about our work
lunch will be provided   the website is now live
the records are not selling   problems are not solved
increasingly invaded   a pattern will emerge

virtual performance   impossible exchange
journey into disability   get experience & support
clowning's a state of playfulness   find the fool within
please explore the writing space   the industrial age of print

promises are hard to keep   that photograph of you
blur of invented metaphor   scales out of true
afterlife or afterwards?   answers in the wind
fumbling with your sweatshirt   shutting up the mind

stolen light or lantern   this studio is mine
now midwinter's been & gone   let's head toward sunshine
prophecy's out of the question   perhaps we'll all pull through
secret societies & brotherhoods   things happen   as they do

Characters From the Past

mosaic of information   economies of time
tools for orientation   spiritual decline
ecstatic individuals   ancestors alive
broken glass & metal   data reassigned

ideal organization   voices that emerge
fearful contact with the dead   lights flashing in your eyes
guile   invention   celebration   magic of every kind
illusion's guiding power   learn to fetishize

preservation of the body   truth reclaimed from lies
future triggered by the past   distant church bells chime
shared languages & borrowed dreams   perceptive metaphors
the deepening of distance   nothing's ever done

limits of containment   a horrid snapping sound
only one possible response   argument run aground
tickertape alter-egos   rumours uncomfirmed
vertical human architecture   waiting to found

Defined by Opposition

a substitute for something real   the same postmodern fog
biting   snapping at the world   images of god
I am not seeing what you are   I am not sure at all
underlining lots of words   settling for 'unreal'

before the sidewalk ceremony   places hard to find
too polite and too restrained   social skills refined
the many futures possible   interactive fiction
how to judge the whole event   value pure & simple

frequent if irregular   index of permission
I have never heard of him   what do you recommend?
what if we were serious?   some real blood might come
little point in quoting   it feels less restrained

privilege now pointless   power remakes the world
people are still children   forever is consumed
watermark upon a bill   accepted as the truth
vacate memory body pack   give us the edge in life

Everyone Else

an interest in art & movies   a pile of broken dreams
flecked with too many colours   laughing til it hurts
searing pain   ripped shoulder   arthritis down below
high hopes & expectations   response learned long & slow

listen to music that you love   learning something new
seriously involved with silence   smoke under the hood
a sign of stubborn insistence   what do you think of change?
identification with the other   angels in their cage

live like a working class hero   gulping down mugs of beer
he too might be a stranger   occasional feelings of fear
better late than never   brawls at closing time
only one pub in the village   level crossing sign

familiar with brilliant freedoms   never playing ball
scorch & crackle & burning   morning's blueness on the wall
I feel the sadness gathering   how does this world endure?
alive with sorrow & lament   now we are even fewer

Food Chain

absolute isolation   days empty by design
an edge   an iridescence   difference & change defined
understanding social space   real people's lives
combine materials produced   jazz on weekday nights

blanks & dots inserted   landmarks along the way
learning to read language   applied geology
certain of the future   gauze where eye should be
mapping the human coastline   mental activity

overburdened by weight of vision   squatting on railway land
rusted bolts on Brunel's bridge   influence & change
the public never consulted   forces outside control
count the cost of trespass   international youth revolt

give everyone permission   control your human face
co-operative decisions   please appear to dance
cognition & perception   introduce yourself
verbal integration   that   for now   is all

Glitter as an Effect of Sight & Sound

jumps about   dances   babbles   first full-time disease
negotiates a crowd of things   do you know where you've been?
dangerous provocation   happenings   ideas
a penny extra for the towel   how privileged you are

there will be no mercy   your curses have backfired
positive & negative   predators removed
long memories   dream commodities   demanding energy
existence has no meaning   form never speaks the truth

a breathless fish come up for air   safe passage to the light
electronic viruses   filtering the void
another world is possible   we must divide our time
cosmic tree on sacred hill   the universe we know

rhetoric   direction   conflict   uncertainty
many things cannot be known   without pondering
complete misunderstanding   lilies of the field
final demolition   a fall of autumn leaves

Hell, a Beginner's Guide to

tangled fear contention   the gap between the wars
learning to kiss mouths   you haven't kissed before
shuffling like a zombie   be satisfied with facts
box to check on census form   infant on your back

meaning through translation   misappropriated dream
obstinate clot of people   who appreciate & believe
guest speakers every speech day   defined & built the world
no compass or guidebooks   ghost maps all they had

the passing of the image   the simulated god
cultural superstition   perpetuated myth
describe the scene as follows   self-mutilation & embrace
dominion of the dying   sacrificial death

twisted loops & endless drones   traditional living space
not his friend or buddy   the audience transformed
regime of complicity   muted talking books
beautiful indifference   the world destroys itself

Investigate the Process

development of new ideas   first cold spark from flints
integrate resources   library's thickened wall
hardcore performance poetry   hope our timing's right
resist being labelled   we should never fight

introduction in the making   imagination fails
process allows creation   blur of a bird's wing
viewing text that disappears   new ideas of space
screens instead of easels   there is a price to pay

excitement because it's tangible   discourse because joined in
salesmen selling stories   charged images of speed
causality is dreamlike   the patterning of streets
a poem shouldn't say too much   depicted not redeemed

hysterical vibrations   branded genetic code
primary threads & qualities   anything but a void
once we circled the present   today we make the world
change attitude & perception   this story is your own

January Morning

silver tide horizon   flooded silver fields
went for a long morning walk   gloves & hat required
remind myself where we now live   why we moved down here
abandoned boats and mudflats   new grass on the quay

wind effects & structures   maps drawn & thrown away
housing works in situ   our conservation zone
fast expanding village   never-ending work
living without tension   collateral damage done

entertain enigmas   friends who never call
same familiar paintings   hung on our new walls
books I love on my shelves   the same old lack of time
no sense of identity   what is or isn't mine

themes & variations   burnt-out nervous state
conversation & discussion   answers in the wind
collapsing ecosystem   don't know who I am
wrote this without flinching   made up my own mind

Know That

there are several known unknowns   the map is still unclear
many call this useless work   they don't have a clue
the fog is finally clearing   you don't have to decide
I try to live life in the past   it turned out rather well

you don't have to have children   you don't have to believe
progress is hindered by secrecy   you can never leave
doesn't matter which route you choose   if you know what you're doing
I am on the waiting list   I still care for you

changed the course of someone's life   bought a house for two
unfamiliar freedoms   curtains twitch as we walk past
fruit in dishes   chairs & table   mirror in the hall
I don't know how   I don't know why   lyric as default

you're my hero   space expands   so does the human mind
tell me you forgive me   that you're coming home
up here in the writing space   someone cares for you
I am in love   I don't get tired   this poem is not true

Languishing in a Motel

fierceness of paper tigers   night terrors & grinding teeth
tornado plane crashing drowning sleepwalking through old dreams
my escape & obsession   rivers clogged with dams
people's love & synergy   blurred handmade taboos

infectious care & attention   what happens when you leave?
can only write emotion   it's something in the genes
independence or rebellion   are distant cousins of mine
sliding toward conclusion   answering chain of command

you became a nostalgia addict   perfect smile of the past
we don't have to be heroes   are what & who we are
the laughter of liberation   certainties dissolve
forget ideas & tradition   the sun came out today

wordplay disguised as an essay   obsessed with text & sound
watercolour postcards   fathers we never found
hurrah for our eviction   obligations up against the wall
the mechanics of illegal squatting   a metaphor for soul

Mournful Delay

reclamation & reconstruction   subsiding into night
revels in abundance   amplified morning light
neurotransmitter chemicals   muttering paranoid threats
most likely sued for libel   no friends   no girls   no pets

airways over the city   not a flying man
the world has little room for him   or new adventure games
flat mundane description   collaboration has begun
work leads to mutation   authorship transformed

indulgent & expensive   black holes on the stage
garish neon lettering   photos on the page
the media our salvation   nothing hard & fast
investigate the process   separate sheep & goats

can sound put things together?   what is going on?
confused on several levels   translate all the poems
early literary history   got drunk   never looked back
things found in a junkyard   lines from other books

Not the Original Ending

disorder threatens order   kind of presupposed
all is true not interesting   however much we know
blend of corruption & promise   attention to design
cosmetic counter specific   intelligent disdain

depart as quietly as possible   ever so eager to learn
fabricated in the basement   disappointed man
gratuitous foreign diction   happiness out of town
in situations of extreme stress   he lights out on his own

textual experiment & shock   the idea of poetic sign
being locked in is unthinkable   too many words around
mind can move & loop & stretch   city's liquid form
mystification got away   it's now a darker world

underdogs in the catastrophe zone   angels sometimes win
universities that encode   formalised extremes
versions of the story   inherited status & power
we need less institutions   more reasons to write home

Open Studio

cold brilliance & glittering eyes   humanity uncertain
space between silence & silence   a stumbling block to all
underlining lots of phrases   too polite & too restrained
reading other people's work   much more could be said

strong words in a wooden box   mostly apt & true
considering relocation   give me a year or two
hibernation or chronic doldrums   frightening at the time
good to have a next-door-nurse   this how I am

enviably large studio space   known through photographs
some engaging encounters   people wandering in
avoiding overdrafts for a year   walking to restaurants
biting & snapping at the world   not too ob-scure or -tuse

not sure what the portrait was   nail the lid down hard
vision blocking tractors   heavenly choir behind
designed to push the boat out   sentences acute
the first one was an interim   this one is the last

Paintstripper

this is a one-page wonder   see my alien life
a multimedia opera   a long involving tale
I want to believe in UFOs   want to find out more
there's a real shortage of idiots   (the opposite is true)

waterbed inertia   rolling seasick dreams
frustration's wider   deeper   the river's just a stream
'stream' is just a part of speech   washing land away
a wealth of new resources   tiny hands at play

we know your views on intention   how change will change this town
don't think of all that heavy stuff   press the button down
don't think of all that heavy stuff   this town has changed with time
plunder texts for language   press the button down

cold damp in my studio   getting used to paint again
words have suddenly run out   colours in the rain
tried to draw by moonlight   evening charcoal grey
the window wasn't even glass   plastic melted right away

Questions Will Be Asked

reach beyond the metaphor   to actual transformation
attempt a kind of portraiture   grasp the instant light
photo image of a star   imprinted on your psyche
all of them good looking   go out & press the flesh

idiotic yet industrial   gigs were such a waste
recurring chord progression   audiences yelled abuse
multimedia panic   autographed CDs
words & images conspire   the story never leaves

old council donkey-jacket   a confused startled look
an end to private property   things moving much too fast
conspiracy & violence   bombs on the top deck
it's not like I want trouble   it just seemed a good idea

I don't know why   or remember how   I simply never cared
always wanted to conquer the world   despite our different tastes
songs with childlike insistence   'oh baby I love you'
not perceived by human gaze   stopped time coming true

Rock & Roll Singer

rowing across the ocean   cast away delight
more drawing & less painting   keep it black & white
information as event   finality of death
something not connected   networks now controlled

no transcendent dimension   all you need is dynamite
confrontation is what counts   space may be torn apart
the banality of music   birds singing for their lives
always state your units   pissed out of his mind

processed by the programme   words best sung aloud
different in performance   ear kept to the ground
I have done all that I can   there's nothing left to know
straight in from the airport   straight on with the show

higher definition   please confirm these dates
spiral & repetition   the rules of its own game
adolescent wonder   jump around and see
in the filter of the void   contradictory

Self Portrait with Bottles & Bricks

composite of figures   horizon in the dark
discursive presentation   magnetic pole of faith
inharmonious state of doubt   fundamental codes
past & future collaborate   destroy skin & thought

disintegration & complexity   cognitive abandon
conceptual deviation   expected content drained
elements of reality   fragments of model proof
imagined grainy footage   ironic whispered truth

labyrinth & enigma   seemingly shared ground
dreams of immortality   self-identity defined
recurring motifs & cartoons   stretched to breaking point
the forger replaces the traitor   can't forget his debt

impossible definitions   the magic of glass rooms
the silhouettes of shadows   endless traffic flows
unreal suspension & silence   the spirit indisposed
we must emerge from exile   build economies of hope

The Geography of Escape

common features of timeslip   landscapes of ice & snow
stone memorials for the dead   romantic restless past
discovery or rediscovery   choice which makes you free
hope & self-determination   pious platitudes

one more in a range of voices   reaction a mistake
intuition & openness   relics & body parts
seeking the buried city   the rhetoric of siege
special forms of language   curses   spells & charms

therapuetic journeys   lamentation for what's gone
mind of sentient viewers   catching up with thought
natural & supernatural   ecstatic reach of mind
powers of recollection   transfigured & renewed

rice & sweets are scattered   plans & systems made
repetition & reality   insidious control
feeling of completion   your place in the world
conditions of existence   slow-creeping final days

Under the Noses of the Powerful

barriers to learning   consumed & cast aside
war   slaughter & madness   the gender gap is large
rest & recreation   implemented schemes
half-remembered favourite songs   new theories of dreams

goals & expectations   you can't run but you can hide
living in a borrowed space   first or second prize
landscapes of the body   production & exchange
simple-seeming textures   a real or proper place

the rich experience of listening   obsessed with coins & bills
story's high-tech promises   brain operates this way
no decision re decisions   corporate free speech
games of appreciation   attempts to catch ideas

entropy & redemption   direct light & empty space
more substantial & lasting   webcams for every taste
secondhand information glut   people on the phone
what makes a story a story?   work either in groups or alone

Vanishing Point

crutch of punctuation   prose whose syntax stinks
anything might happen   poetic hyperlinks
calvinist mentality   noise of remembered war
perceived from certain angles   geometry of desire

recognized as landscape   exclude semantic codes
address rules & procedures   forget all you know
shades of previous owners   sunsets of single days
shaping urban experience   structuring the world

memories of childhood   feeble time machine
hurt shinbone or elbow   variations on a theme
profane diagnostics   astonishing to hear
what happens in a sentence?   why publish work at all?

borrowing & lending   personal feelings of guilt
inflection & distortion   maybe I've missed the point
illusionistic context   crux of social change
tide moves backwards & forwards   there is no master-plan

Writing to an Audience

the merits of distortion   art from the mundane
fending off your questions   coming back to words
flames punctuate the village   good does not always win
we are our own worst enemies   landscape & weather blend

order from disorder   self-identity as life
priorities reconsidered   attitudes repaired
issues put in context   observe ambition's pain
resist intended meaning   boundaries blur again

a sense of play & pleasure   sky seems to be on fire
banter & strange stories   forgotten proper names
although useful if considered   facts make little change
both sides of the border   old memories survive

antithesis of balanced sound   weakens the support
impromptu drive   suspended road   swerve into goodbye
characteristic disturbance   sign your name in ink
memes beneath the surface   culture   myth & rhyme

Xoanon

walking barefoot in the morning   writing songs about the moon
formal elements of composition   stop us being moved
production & consumption   impact of the sign
cultural condition   the way we think & talk

attempts to resurrect history   consistently miss the point
create a speaking body   with standard speaking parts
dignified occasion   there's nothing more to say
never is always a long time   instantly replayed

cars are in the distance   acquiring interpersonal skills
noise is sometimes echoed   voice sometimes replies
music overspills intention   sound remains intact
a good deal less pretension please   what we need are facts

enter into public debate   grab me by the neck
mechanical aids are encouraged   submissions should be sent
note that I've said nothing   this will end too soon
rudimentary business   songs about the moon

Youngster

a certain pattern promised   a circle still concealed
ash & bone on shoreline   dancing out-of-breath
bubblegum in playground   a calendar of kids
cosmic pebbles & diamond dreams   crocuses in flower

there are devils in my attic   conscience has disappeared
old habits in a sunbeam   dried-out paper leaves
fiery plume at sunset   rain collected in a pool
tiny evergreen footprints   songs that make god dance

words in perpetual motion   music's sacred sound
tumbleweed & corral   sourdough & playhouse gold
a miracle   a guiding hope   intersecting paths
perfumed dust & sunlight   no-one else is home

house absorbing moonlight   all of me is gone
destiny & promises   rainbows   raindrops   stars
remember me   remember me   whispers resurrection
dance on wormwood rafters   in the country of desire

Zealous

old man in a snowy field   with sculptures that he made
sings a blacksmith's rusting song   a widower's lament
tanktotem one   tanktotem two   here is the welder's heart
star clusters & star cages   neutered barbed wire fence

interior   exterior   clean welded edges   time
seeks immediate solution   plunges & expires
infinite number of ideas   drawn with steel in air
an aptitude to improvise   bending light & time

open construction   rusted lines   metal miracles
fist fight articulation   had no time for fools
spraypainted sketches   shorthand draw   breaking his own rules
echoes of rural childhood   stacked up shiny cubes

questioned all his critics   trusted no-one else
intensity of feeling   eloquence of form
terminal iron landscape   heart in the right place
always sought honest response   making art his home

Spray Painting in the Dark

Crease Patterns
for Rachel Blau DuPlessis

there is a place for any poem before it is written
    the gender question torques translation
      riddles solved are now more complex
              a coffee cup and a doughnut are the same
   I use standard notation plus a few arrows
just rough hewn floor boards and shelves
         physically cut and staple it to new pages
    to get a workable sequence
        a poem in which words fail

   paperfolding for play was known by a variety of names
     the word was adopted in kindergartens
I am waiting for a book from the remote storage facility
      some gluing and cutting may be allowed
a sentence of a looping temporality
  fold here
      among the ark of random things
      here   & here
       boulder is round rock
   a sentence of looping temporality

    pick a point on the crease pattern
       something that wraps the eye
  how many creases originate at this vertex?
small squares of paper top and bottom
    is it possible to have an odd number of creases?
how about the relationship between mountain and valley folds?
     poetry is made of words
  newsprint, newspaper, phone book pages,
      used copy and computer paper
can you have a vertex with only valley folds?
   lay bare the fragments and displacements found
    flashes, fragmentations, and erasures
       the page is never blank
    how many changes will it take?
a way to think and undertake understanding
   the page is never blank

original creations and diagrams
how about the angles around this point?
even minor differences can be confusing
memory, history, and language itself
was poetry always now impossible?
many secular or worldly customs require
being chained to the cosmos
pure information and different textual elements
ears behind the head
why should anything be written or not?
the page is never blank

regimes of complete astonishment
the processual construction of a space of discourse
unnerving in lack of detail
playing with textures of memory
a formative and generous gift
none of the poems is perfect
I ended up completely beguiled

Beauty is in the eye of the folder

Arizona Sister Butterfly

one of those days when you find yourself thinking
about whether or not you are thinking clearly
sort of like those floating islands made of recycled soda cans
a stylistic and philosophic laboratory
shifting frames of reference
disruptive and disorienting
shimmer and burn
they ignited fast and extinguished just as quickly
shimmer and burn

scaling the building
toward a new understanding
whatever you wish   real or imagined
the most brilliant thing to be doing
high gravity, high temperatures
a different frequency
feel clever for absorbing it

longing becomes tangible and observable
does it never rain in certain parts of the city?
everyone wants to breathe and nobody can
a gusto and charm all of its own
put your heart and soul on a plate
orange lights in the night
conversation with the past
seeing well ahead
long sweeping passages
a smouldering broken heart

think of a busy intersection
transport systems that animate a city
follow intricate turns of thought
and unravel
imposture is based on anonymity
how little has changed

This is made of glass – we can't see it in the dark

Jazz Heart Electric

a city of words
not been heard since
a map of the place where mind and heart intersect
arranged in a deeply moving way
meaning through difference
patterns of recognition change
solitary companion
a stranger who walks past every day

acute visibility
coiled up   convuluted   ready to spring
these things have no connection
shadowy explanations and shadowy emotions
all sorts of illusions
surprise gets in the way

increasing speed of life
echoed in brevity
foregrounded sound reflects increasing cacophony
echoed in brevity
make the most of small spaces
collage an extension of juxtaposition
echoed in brevity

see the ragged margin
elsewhere as a labyrinth
a scene upon which another is quickly superimposed
a faculty of listening
each composition slowly becomes visible
as in any maze

You just know it will sound awesome live

Paper Securities

motorways in the rain
offices with empty shelves
the sound of diesel engines in the dark
no show students

recognising the celestial highs
`an art form all in itself`
fast moving sun
a magpie with a beak full of orange peel flies overhead
wet light glinting on the grid of coloured cars
on the roof of the multi-storey

`the grass is always greener`
break language down from simple narrative use
labyrinths are everywhere
jolting awake in just the right way
the impression of conversations with an angel
scattered debris among the ruins
we're living the answer even now
terrified of returning home
there is no mistaking or escaping the author

my photo on the wall two hundred miles from home

Only One Animal Was On My Mind

he communicates through language
growling should be taken very seriously
a lot of things going on at once
a curmudgeonly collection of materials and ideas
an old geezer's speech therapy tool box
sensible wait in the wings   working silently in the background
everybody is tired of us getting up on the podium

these forms aren't meant to scare you or anything
the chaos laboratory
can make the world seem more threatening than before
a continual shift between vertical and horizontal
sound & sense should always be preserved
ultimately theory is a means to an end
dust in the light

a whole raftful of friends with cups of tea
ready to contemplate the popular
each character should choose an obsession
mad scientists pioneered the first wave of assault on human boredom
not just a flesh wound
an original, rebellious spirit
history understood in a very profound way

a place where silence endures as an enveloping presence

Full Given Name Is Not Set Forth

these are ones to watch out for
           the names of God in the Old Testament
     expressions of the divine spirit
                visions for the future of our company
                          no matter how harsh the conditions

              this is the case of the chroniclers   of writers
       moot to discuss what constitutes inner and outer reality
              an illegal playground for us
the problem with bubbles is that no one knows when they have popped
     keeps slipping through one's fingers
                           just beyond one's grasp

          it is cheaper to bring it in than it is to drill for it
                the distance we have to travel
reminds us of our immediate and impending departure
                each of us begins in the middle
      wariness and distance begin to soften towards the end
          all attractions can be reached by using a detour route
                        the urge toward judgement is absent

      multiple degrees of excitement, curiosity and sweet confusion
          a new voice from collaborations
                      states of illuminated insight
        the mysteries of character and fate
                happen in memory and the imagining
     something startling occurs in the ending
         making its own kind of promise
         poems will not be returned

          May it all end with stout covers

Secret Lifes

'It is necessary to speak of the ghost . . .'
—Paul Morley

for Bill & Yan

The Secret Life of Anger

Shotgun wedding solemn tryst,
allophanic scramble of the world.

The discovery of photography,
a kind of excuse for a lie.

A site where choices are made,
constant negotiations with words

that never keep their promises.
The language of self-questioning,

time's involuntary flashbacks.
Walking alone through the storm.

The Secret Life of Books

Threshold spaces: the social
place of a text on the shelf.

I have a genuine interest in
traditions of dead generations,

am trying to find a new sentence
in the real city of language,

a shared vocabulary. What
is the author writing about?

A very inexact apocalypse,
on a particular kind of day.

The Secret Life of Children

Days are spent in small houses
with coloured books, mapping

the movements of rabbits and dogs,
rolling model cars down plastic ramps.

Everyone has a collection of acorns
and pretty stones from the beach,

each takes their turn to wear
angel wings, high heels,

sparkly dresses and scarves,
breathe wonder into the world.

The Secret Life of the Creek

Very high tide. Water overspills,
restructures the entire village.

Acknowledging river's existence,
we drive along the upper road,

remember our garage is full
of canoes. This time of year,

the creek's a felt presence we
start to understand, journey

a diversion and a lesson,
a new economy of habitation.

The Secret Life of the Dead

Tombstones and signposts,
terrible things that happened.

Owing death to the world,
he wasted time going native,

a slow life slowed down
to promote the unutterable,

embracing a religion
of resentment and denial.

Compulsive nomads, we still
traverse the desert of time.

The Secret Life of Despair

Garbled conversation,
obsession and noise:

impatient navigation
of memory and names

using only old charts.
The living are already dead,

shut up in windowless houses,
scattering abandoned names,

burying their parents alive;
looking for truth in the dark.

The Secret Life of My Father

Model trains in boxes in the loft,
local history papers on his desk.

Photos of now-demolished buildings,
a foundation stone from the rubble.

Unreadable notes towards a book
full of not-to-be-forgotten facts.

That day is not yet here. The situation
has changed. My now long-gone father

has turned to tears and remembering,
an awkwardly choreographed embrace.

The Secret Life of the Igloo

The rich future I imagine for myself
is a blizzard of internal monologue

and empty white horizons. Half-blind,
eyes closed against the cold sunlight,

I try to define a presence, wander
between possessions and passions.

But what's the point, me telling you
about it if you can see for yourself?

On the information superhighway
there is no room for ice or snow.

The Secret Life of the Kayak

Stimulant hover, heroic wilt.
Whispers, exhibitions, rain

pouring from our gutters
down toward the creek.

Now I am on the trail.
Sideways for storage,

topsyturvy on the car,
pushed off from the mud.

A kind of heaven, paddling
alone in a field of water.

The Secret Life of the Light

Hangs around all day not worrying,
dying for a hearty slice of the action.

Bounces off mirrors, through fibre optic bends,
seeps into our bedroom from the street outside,

pushing the dark away. Doesn't care if it's
an outdated metaphor, just wants to shine.

Particle or wave? Another forgotten problem.
Rituals and performance, multiple meanings:

the physics of the spirit world is anathema
to the spirits of the physical world.

The Secret Life of Mist

Real dreams of city life,
the royal road to knowledge.

Religious ritual or dreamtime:
low cloud across the creek.

No clear sense of location,
the burden of awareness and place.

Listening at a distance
to neighbours in the park,

walking back home with
eyes both open and shut.

The Secret Life of Music

Ear to the ground,
memories surface

as music enters:
childhood moments,

limits of containment
in historical sequence.

Fragmented epiphanies,
particular sounds;

personal soundtracks
to private worlds.

Secret Life of the Plumber

Tentative sacraments: tributes read aloud,
his poem scattered with her ashes out at sea.

Told me he'd done time. Someone else said he'd
volunteered for two months after the earthquake hit,

simply picked up his tools and went, leaving his
studio, his partner, his home. Still doesn't talk

about it much. Spends time painting over mirrors,
deconstructing string theory, swallowing dark pints.

Talks to anyone who will listen, stares into the pool
he built in the garden from discarded local stone.

The Secret Life of Polemic

An unending stream of deceptive signals,
opinion spluttering like a coffee machine.

You could call it compulsion or vitriol,
a personal crusade or an ongoing debate.

I have spent a lot of time thinking
about argument and have concluded

the opposite is true. Where is meaning,
interpretation, evaluation and expression?

Whisper to preserve my secret: I am
well aware of my own world view.

The Secret Life of Rain

Depressed. Staring into rain
beyond the playroom doors.

Autumn is earlier than ever:
smoke is mist is cold is grey.

Miles from nowhere, especially
work and home, I am drowning.

Language problem if the doctor calls:
no reply. Other storms and places

weave in and out of memory.
I have no idea how this happened.

The Secret Life of the Sky

Even on the darkest night the moon is around
in the land of unintentional melodrama and love,

a dramatic monologue waiting to soon happen.
Star's secret light slips into the room through the blinds,

paper textures stand out: tones of beige and bone
briefly appear, synthesized out of air's worn edges.

A woman on the other side of the mountains and you
before the glacier. Gold and silver clouds in the flowing

water, darkness in the soil. A single frog visits our pond,
unaware how many colours are in tonight's painted sky.

The Secret Life of the Skylight

I am planning the afterlife
through a square of glass.

The clouds sometimes help:
dreams have to be made,

not chanced upon. Out of
reading time, I have drifted

into condensation's arms
for much of the afternoon,

a double-glazed glance
through distant doorways.

The Secret Life of Thunder

A sailboat in a tiny pond.
The temperatuire of water.

Away from lightning's flash,
my life is lived outdoors,

a tall and neon privilege
lost in a strange country.

Between storm's shout and silence,
a temporary moment of closure,

a new form of accommodation.
I am returning home to die.

The Secret Life of the Treehouse

Forward tilt: building castles
on the beach, half my life ago,

we dreamed a shed on stilts
into being, cut back the trees

so that it would fit. Now,
wisteria climbs the supports,

acorns drop on the roof. Dawn
sees visits from foxes and cats.

Childhood's a ghost I want
my daughters to embrace.

The Secret Life of the Village

It has almost stopped raining,
but cloud's still lower than our house.

Abandoned shoes and burn marks
show points of departure on the street,

blackberries and sloes fill the hedges,
waders call at night. I used to have

a bookcase that opened out on hinges
to reveal a secret room beyond.

If there is such a thing as community
it is now invisible in the morning mist.

A Fire in the House of Ice

after Mario Merz

Lines on the Point of Disappearing

'The only possible representation of panic is velocity'
 —Mario Merz

Instructions: to think.

•

To read that which is not written.

•

Concentration visible:
an igloo the ideal form.

•

How twisted and strange our toddler's sentences
as she struggles to say what she means. I'm bored
by continual reference to language and meaning.

•

Words always lead to others,
notes refer to other books:

endless signposts pointing
everywhere and nowhere,

open maps for the intrigued.

•

Buildings, streets, cars and parking lot;
bundles of twigs, roots and flower.
Miracle of order and articulation
dropped in as a kind of shorthand.

The igloo developed from secret knowledge
that came suddenly on a long winter Sunday.
I desired to make art that shone like the outback,
to come up with a metaphor never used before.

•

How can I attend to so little for so long?
I fetch tradition and carry it with me.
Meanwhile, sentences glimmer over igloos
built in the counter-tradition of landscape.

At the same time all the world I know
hails my initiative, toasts my success.
The stones and the lead are necessary;
space is important, this space is fluid.

It is necessary to look at the complexity of life;
a steep metal staircase winds round the outside.
Grace is that mix of fullness and lightness,
those privileged moments of existence –

moments of writing, circumstance or love.

•

If there were red concrete I would build a red igloo.
As it is, I have slate, stone and mud, withies, and steel,
have canvas and wax, lead and sheet glass,
light to caulk joints between outside and in.

Dark associations and mythical allusions
are embedded in detailed manipulations
of impulse and import. I have the impression
that I have invented an art form which breathes,

that is restless, knowledgeable, savage
and spiritual. It has severe health problems
and a library of books I'm never tired of,
although I wish we had more shelves.

Where has the weather gone? May as well ask
about higher meaning or bringing the reader
closer to the lyric voice of the poet. It is only
hours away from the North Pole by plane.

Instructions: Make an enormous effort.
Say no to the theatricality of a situation.
Don't shut the door, you'll let the air in.
Try to be led astray. You may think I am

teaching my grandma to suck eggs. I'm not.

•

What one reads on one's own notebook page
is the slime trail left by time, a snail spiral
through culture, highlighting narrative and
attempting to reduce it to manageable size.
There is a compulsion to sacrifice everything
or frame it on the wall. The movement of
animals is defined by rules of growth, their
simple desire to feed and inhabit the earth.
We can clip stone to the spine and neon
to the frame, but the ensuing tension
between moved and unmoved, spectator
and maker will not bring about a solution.
Please note the after image, the faint
stain of the *my-oh-my-is-that-what-we-did-
in-those-days?* upon memory's headline.
Order is always waiting in the future to
meet us: out come all the imaginary tigers.

In verse one I tried to point to a problem
that cannot be resolved. All of us have had
the experience of trying to do nothing –
stop busyness and vacuity pours through,
red sap rising as far as the branches.
This is not enemy propaganda, it is the
culmination of glacier's lifelong drift.
The melting ice threatens to be every
moment, a wound that will not heal.
We have not done any work at all,
have simply thought about how
our lives could be. But here come
the grey weeks of work to weigh us down
before we find translucence and inertia.
Now in our village with the falling light,
neatly-carved blocks of ice surround us
where we have built our igloo homes.

A Fire in the House of Ice

Igloo was made
by drawing a circle

around the circle
along the circle

diameter and dome
joined to one another

archway slanted
down to the outside

a piece of lake
for a window

wind could blow
over but not into

No fires
not much firewood

some driftwood
close to the sea

Frozen water would
keep the heat in

stone gardens
animate flesh

From cold memory
new figures rise

Follow move to follow
other places in the world

A piece of ice
Igloos to build

Child's Play

Child's play! Building an igloo is easy,
building an igloo is easy and fun,
and the igloo is fun. And your igloo
is a great place to spend the the night.

Stuck in the mountains, in a shelter such
as an igloo, heavy, cold air can be diverted
away from the occupants by digging a cold sink
to channel the air down and away this winter.

With warmth inside the igloo, cold falls away.
The surface of the igloo at the edge of the shore
is frozen ice. You are somewhere else. Stay,
stay overnight. Sleep under the Northern Lights,

under the stars in a snow or glass igloo. What
an experience! Do you know about the amazing
potential energy source known as cold fusion?
See smoke coming out of nowhere, the thin air.

This poem is a new commission that explores
movement and stillness in nature. The igloo
lets stillness in, which is sometimes the difference
between life and death. The igloo is a great death.

It works along similar principles to photomontage,
creating a new image out of whatever was put in.
This prevents snow from blowing into the igloo,
offers you pixelated detail in the foreground.

Welcome to my igloo, a habitat for homeless listeners
of avant-garde music which we assume has meaning.
The igloo tool lets you build an igloo out of an igloo;
as the frozen wind howls outside, inside you are toast.

An igloo is made this way because it is the way it is made,
is the only thing to build with cubic enclosure on a pole.
It forms a smooth, airtight surface: the igloo is a great
structure, easily constructed out of snow in hours.

From the outside of the igloo you might expect to find
eskimos inside. There are not. Inside the building is
a fireplace. If you light a fire within an igloo it will melt.
Instantly. The igloo will be formally opened to the sky.

This so-called igloo of ours is not perfectly straight.
Made with sheets of glass, so you can see inside,
it is a complete embarrassment. Some days I don't want
to be seen crawling out of the entrance. Send a message

to the captain: detonate and destroy. The smoke from inside
the ruin will be popular with small children. Warming is hitting
the igloo trade but there is no problem if you leave and prefer
to strengthen global connections between peoples of the world.

To the igloo from whence we came for more fun and games –
let's continue the adventure! The igloo remains compartment
-alized and highly classified. Do you know what an igloo is yet?
This is my igloo, the igloo I made for my kindergarten class.

More moths than you can shake a leg at. Strange warming trends.
I am thankful for igloo builders, and have put boxes of snow
in the shed for later use. It is a moral position when you
think of it, designed for the long-term storage of doubt.

There is no problem if you are someplace else, so take a step
backwards, leave the ultimate dream and control that mouth.
Step away from the igloo. Notice the tourists in the background,
the revolving door. This translucent dome is beauty overgrown.

BIRTHDAY
for Natasha

My eighth year in the igloo of parenthood.
Outside, autumn has arrived with the rain;
we won't be able to visit the beach today.

Is it isolation in a room of books, or wholeness
in the bosom of the family? She seems to love
her presents but is overwhelmed by possibilities

and choice. Do we want her to grow up quickly
or play with her dolls? Why is she so contrite?
And why won't her baby sister stop screaming?

So many questions stay unanswered; time
simply passes as the ice melts. It gets dark
and the neighbours are back a week early;

they got robbed on the motorway in Spain,
couldn't stick the thought of staying away.
New toys are in boxes in the dining room,

pushed to the centre while we paint the walls.
Is the off-white too lemon or the yellow too
sunny? Do the dents in the plaster still show?

We don't care any more. We need to unpack
and put some family history on the shelves,
move books and records out of the garage.

The future turns up early, we do not miss the past;
the igloo shrinks as we and the children get older.
How quickly these words melt on to the page.

Double Act

New challenges and ideas. Contradictions
cut with glass, ways to exceed expectation:
these two strangers should definitely meet.

Fame is a spiral of meaning and thought;
discarded newspapers and forgotten science
the key to making things. An escape artist

hangs above the audience in a moment
of upside-down crucifixion. Time swings
him like a pendulum towards freedom –

he will wriggle his way into the future
and emerge rubbing back the circulation
in his arms. Illusion cannot be clear cut.

Neon lights up the world here, sequences
of numbers between slabs of stone and
steel frames: shelters not for sheltering.

Our contradictions are broken glass; we find
ways to change fixed opinion. Hidden keys
and tricks of light lead to bigger shows,

where Mario Merz and Harry Houdini co-star.
Fiction is fact and fame is hope kept alive.
In the glass igloo day is always with you.

Download

The desire to enter an igloo is entirely instinctive.
There's no end to the delightful possibilities inside.
Music's in the aether, pouring down onto disc –
so much for the grasping, so much for the asking.

In our igloo, life has melted into a unique shape:
ambiguity in the first place (written on pencil or leaves),
numbered stairs in ascending order (difficult to climb),
and unnumbered stars outside (impossible to count).

It's such an undertaking, experiencing the complex
whilst trying to ride this wall of death. Sandbags and ice,
piles of newspapers, gathered brushwood, steel cage –
building what is not possible is quite a task.

There's no need to keep going on about ice houses,
it's all been done and dusted, tried and tested.
Reading what is not written asks the reader to join in,
shows the mathematical progression of human need.

Igloo, Do We Go Around Houses, Or Do Houses Go Around Us?

Fluid as figurative as any form,
pouring into the neon fountain.

Firehoses and ferment, the feel
of the day before it really begins.

I'm fine, you're furious. We find
ourselves a future to light up

and try to make a fragile path,
a visible trace of script in the sky.

Igloo
i.m. Robert Lax

Inside becomes outside; it is as grey
as day can be and as light as night
often is, depending on the season
and how wide your eyes are open.

It is dark outside now Robert
is no longer here. Words splinter
until we learn to read them,
islands of shadow on the page.

No escaping from or shelter in
the cold igloo we call death:
corridors of glass and snow,
stone memories pegged in place.

Outside seeps inside; it is as light
as it will ever be. You've slipped
away and I will never visit.
How wide-eyed alive you seem.

Monochrome

No matter how complex
the shape of the igloo

this structure moves
toward simplification,

a space within a landscape:
hiding places we had as children,

a certainty of being protected
from whatever happens outside.

This is not minor or distant news,
this is immediate sensation.

AD REINHARDT AT THE NORTH POLE
for Dennis Milner

        nothing more than a black square on a white field
nothing more than a black square on a white field
        nothing more than a black square on a white field
nothing more than a black square on a white field
        nothing more than a black square on a white field
nothing more than a black square on a white field
        nothing more than a black square on a white field
nothing more than a black square on a white field
        nothing more than a black square on a white field
nothing more than a black square on a white field
        nothing more than a black square on a white field
nothing more than a black square on a white field
        nothing more than a black square on a white field
nothing more than a black square on a white field
        nothing more than a black square on a white field
nothing more than a black square on a white field
        nothing more than a black square on a white field
nothing more than a black square on a white field
        nothing more than a black square on a white field
nothing more than a black square on a white field
        nothing more than a black square on a white field
nothing more than a black square on a white field
        nothing more than a black square on a white field
nothing more than a black square on a white field

This Appendix

sheds no light on what you have just read.
It does not reference properly, clarifies nothing;
it is just a mass of information filling pages.

It may be a useful tool for dramatic purposes,
challenging mythical and historical contexts;
may even be the real substance of the poem.

There is no general critical agreement about this.
The deliberately awkward syntax often employed
by the author suggests the mind's inner gropings:

by means of compressed and patterned language,
in pursuit of beautiful things, life demands
the cultivation of a sudden sense of strangeness.

Begin with the language of utter desolation,
culminate in doom-laden intonation before
returning to the ground of your true being.

It is important how you package your ideas,
to feel the desperation and tension to sell.
Textual transformation is my ace in the hole:

the sacred text is not a sacred text, revision
allows the formation of unresolved reconciliations,
swells of love and compassion, sweet afterbeats.

One reviewer thinks it is all an elaborate joke.
A person who dislikes my work will be very sorry
he was ever born, although I am not one

to take offense. Welcome to my igloo,
come in and share my fish. You would
be wrong to take the above too literally.

Pre-Fab

At night in the courtyard, the deer sings,
as though a songbird sitting on its cage.

The metal skeleton contains a nest,
casts a shadow on the old stone walls.

Loops of light, fragments of plate glass,
frozen fountains: there is a need

for observation and affection.
On its own this all means nothing,

is the outcome of a failed experiment
to build new homes for my people.

Social and psychic experience
can make a man blind, but

this igloo is irresistably beautiful,
a ribbed and rounded articulation.

Selected Evidence

1. Letter Received

Dear R,

Think of a snowball spinning –
what is the correlation with hope?
You may end up someplace else
if spin doesn't create doubt.

The revolving door of order waits in the distance,
a collision of simple biography with abstract thinking.
Form is a difficult animal for me (I am thankful for this),
a strange arrangement of objects we assume has meaning.

Maybe random isn't as random as it used to be?
Conversation evolves as naturally as an igloo
and I think I hear that shadow train a-comin' . . .
All the best from the blue beyond to the way out blue.

    Your friend, P

PS What do you mean by 'embodied'?

2. Letter Sent

Dear P,

I've dropped the ball and lost the game.
Human intelligence develops; cognition
is a highly embodied or situated activity
which can imposes a sense of tension.

Embodied faith believes that paying lip-service
to spiritual ideas isn't enough; embodied faith
insists that believers get their hands dirty.
There is no place where we cannot be human.

Random seems as random still to me, though
I'm interested in your ideas for ordering colour
and words. Toxic flowers fill the landscape
in which areas of our memory are mapped.

    Best wishes, R

PS I hope you're feeling less blue.

The Me and the Here and the Now

'Yes, but every now and then I have my own melancholy.'
—Mario Merz

So the music and books don't matter
but clothes and television do? Build
igloos of self and consumption and
forget everybody else. They can fish
for themselves and see the winter out.
Different memories may have not
even survived, moments flow in such
peculiar ways. I am interested in work
that comes from the studio I carry with me,
am drawn toward a spiritual atheism
which means I don't have to pray or
argue for the love of higher meaning
in my work. Here are some random
openings: the door, the gate, the crack
in the wall, the gap between ceiling
and floor. Simply articulated noise
rings in my ears again and again.

In verse one I tried to substantiate
the link between inner and outer,
discuss the syntax of boundaries,
the patterns of spaces and marks.
I am obsessed with ice and snow,
the way colour fades as you move
between uncertain boundaries,
places where whites and blues
are a two-dimensional remnant
of polar exploration. Were those
early explorers brave and fearless,
single-minded and brave, or just
privileged and foolish men we've
recreated behind layers of the past,

shared dreams open to interpretation?
It is the gaze rather than the breath;
experience is not always life-affirming.

•

I am teaching my grandmother
to suck eggs, leading her astray.
We are family fugitives, hiding out
of harm's way. Huge drifts of snow

are piling up outside, creating
surface effects which distract us
from our tasks. In the same way
that we don't choose our dreams,

I keep finding colour sensations
in the bathroom's mirrored wall:
traces of former occupants, images
that reflect the changing horizon

as sun finally dips out of view
after several long months of day.
Light seeps, retreats and bleeds,
fingers and refingers the world.

It is like entering a dark room
from the bright outside; the way
a leaf, a drop of water or square
of shadow attracts the roving eye.

If there was time I would see red.

•

In the tradition of refiguration
and surprise, I climb the staircase
that spirals around my life. One of
the aims of art is to build bridges

between opposites, give us a new
interpretation of place. But pieces
do not always fit together, and we
must mind the gap between history

and place. When the snow comes,
obscuring the morning's glinting glass,
we hope it will settle, grab scarves
and gloves and rush into the garden.

An igloo is just that: an igloo.

•

The restless mind desires trembling,
does not understand the objects
which it sees or makes. The igloo
is a space that is absolute in itself,

a motionless subject. Selected evidence
is available to view, several analogies
drive the poem along. Stopped moments
of interlocking gazes freeze the day.

•

The rules of growth demand change;
the igloo dissolves the architecture,
encourages us to wonder and question.
Description can be a constant adventure,
resurrection never seemed so unpromising.

•

I am full of the drift of cold air,
have wet socks and shoes from
walking to the shed and back.

•

Lines break where syntax ends: corridors
that connect one thing with another.

•

Memories of emotion and thought.

•

We could live without any sense of ending.

Flipping the Script

Angel Trap

Honey trap, word trap, angel trap,
baited with diagrams and glyphs:
pictures to seduce the aether,
glue language to the page.

Standing still in a sea of words
I sense a pleasant corrosion.
Confusion is rusting away, I
am drowning in possibility.

The sheer strength of the interface
disrupts the link. Each gesture is
deliberate, designed to assassinate
meaning, keep the magic working.

Everything is rumour, everything
is up for grabs. The blank sheet
of paper glows white, appears
to be illuminated from within.

I told no-one about the candles
or the light in the glass of milk.
The body remembers even when
the mind forgets. Which in my case

is quite often. Words have a history,
they come to us from former words,
other worlds. The only way to effect
a rescue is personal participation.

All connections have been severed.

Aroma Fatigue

Words make no sense
We've an abundance
of small satisfactions
face-centred moments
temporary cleavage failure

Maximum acceptable fledglings
new in the father's brood
The earth has mixed up
texts and memories together
Leave well alone

The girl is past her youth
seeks something noncommital
Nonstressed components
magnitude and phase
Now winter comes along

Dreams of fire and light
transparent distribution
a little tinder on the coals
Clears his fields this spring
close to confidence

The moment arrives
like climbing up a slide
A voice whispers in his ear
The more rapid the quench
the more makeshift diffusion

Torchlight dislocation
pearlite reaction
Fears what he cannot see
Her teeth, her tongue
the hardness of the apple

You live in a magic garden

At Home

To be at home in obituaries,
crematoria and car crashes is one thing.
To want for epiphanic endings, love,
desire and wet dreams is another.
I pile the personal archive high,
lay my moonstruck memories low.

Past my sell-by date, I sense a world
chirpily compact and semi-delirious,
full of the latest hopscotch rumours.
Diamond head exposed to the light,
mind a minefield of unravellings,
I count a billion possible regrets.

I lied in my first paragraph, and have
postponed the tentative exploration
to see if I still am. Your chuffedness
is contagious, though I can't bear
the thought of icy roads, all that
wear and tear before the start of day.

Messing with the gospel as given,
a deft equator reimagining rhyme,
the merry colours turn to grey, attracting
frou frou artifacts of a fringe subculture.
Adding mystery to mystery doesn't help,
confusion here goes all the way through.

Consider This My Accidental Suicide Note

Collapsing in a collapsible evening,
your talk breaking down to pieces,

choking it to blue bruises,
hesitant ghosts forced me to see

I don't care for you. That was all,
that's it, all things considered:

touching time, imaginary moons,
and no longer so awfully grateful.

Counterfeit Word Jar
for rob mclennan

Each new word having the final say.
Places no one would feather duster
or think to look. Oh, what a bust,

bit of a counterfeit lemon curd jar,
no longer open or undisturbed,
unaffected by the particulars of change.

Where were you when I started speaking?
You wouldn't believe me if I told you.
I'm still here recognising familiar marks,

learning in the end what the cost is,
making molehills out of mountaineers.
Even trends are no longer fashionable.

I refuse to believe premonitions I've had.
I say that we is all accidental, with only
the faintest outline putting out a thin finger.

Smart deck-chair monkeys keep their mouths shut,
standing to hope again. Not even this is constant;
I have entered the ranks of the anonymous.

You, once you hit something, break it:
lines so sharp, embedded in clean skin.
I means it, she says, it's a hell of a date.

Screeching laughter leaves the faintest scar,
helter-skelter haemorrhage would sacrifice you
on the telephone. I want to call, restless whilst idle.

I calculate association so it must be true.
When was the last time you saw charred bone?
No going back, nine-times-nine days have gone.

Step away to leave until she gets back
and you, too, begin to jump and swirl,
dreaming months beyond reconstruction.

Co-operative random slacker of self & epic proportion,
I would like to dedicate a life supply of hangovers to you.
I'll lighthouse rough earth, become impossible to hurt.

Please, I have long intent for another thirty years:
compelling, awe-inspiring & masterful; an end
on top of another one. I can't slow down just yet.

Cross-Purposes

Walking diagonally across the striped road,
on the way to somewhere else, I sometimes
wish for progression, although stasis moves
in its own way: buzz and hover of the same,
repeated until it grates or is made new,
slowly assumes a different if similar form.

The long sad hoot of clarinet amid electronics,
the clunk and echo of sound as drums kick in
and move the piece along; the desert drift
of quiet sand dunes; windswept fallen leaves.
Part of me is crying out for something more
alive than this cold blue music you adore.

The poetic shimmer, if not abundant,
is enough to light things up. Write is all
I ever do, although my raisin bread works well.
I never actually map out books, the thought
of submitting fills me with dread. I don't
like conversation or talking to the dead.

During the toasted teacake ritual, a re-think.
Enlightenment follows just as day follows night.
I trust my features to assume a sane expression,
dust them down and refresh them with oil,
hoping no-one is watching. All I am saying
is careful how you walk that long thin line.

Dedicated to Compulsion

The sound of your skin, shadows, grief,
and my hair cut just so, surprise you.
I turn around, know exactly who I am

and you know after the mirror tells me
wish again. Kiss it and say *encore*.
I think I could keep up with you now.

That's the funny thing about perception,
you can't see where two worlds touch.
You are the one-who-fights-shadows,

that's why I walked across your back,
grey and white body refusing to rise,
turning white, silver, the way needs do.

It's like I'm firing back at the world,
charging more than I could afford –
or so you said sometimes. But I

was hungry among bare branches,
her bed empty at dawn, a hand on me,
asleep, athirst for the world to stop

or pain to speak. No one could say
a poem, someone else will figure it out,
strut away buzzing and booming.

Burn all your notebooks. A small fire
under your pillow opens the heart
up to light and gives it its song.

Discontinuity

Faith is just one way
to try and preserve the boundaries
we make from imagination.

We stack up the future
using the present tense,
ignoring other permutations.

The world's okay but I want change:
living is an exploratory now,
that the twitch of poetry shows us,

a collage of interruption and argument,
multiple voices and stories,
the crackle of other events.

It's best not to know the way
as we grab out for tomorrow
and trip up over the noise,

best to fabricate discontinuity
and take pleasure in the flow.
Be careful of stillness,

the shift of shadows and light;
beware the darker sense of things.
At day's edge is the doorway to joy.

Entangled
for Allen Fisher

nomad skulk and undercover
different models of oblivion
optional song and science

note held nerve-end high
street curve and circuit twitter
chaotic short-change signal

desire to feel everywhere
devoted future threshold
ultimate form of healing

virtuous noise asymmetry
dark sedimentary layer
assumed grammar's sludge

lured into data theory
imagination and memory
many levels of found text

translation's mistakes manifest
never our mother tongue
paradise not located here

in gravity's orbit I met my match
and fell in to expression trap
one version of the event

several days out to explore
temperature and storm damage
making so much of right now

explanation lost in consideration
shifting attraction of language
a few paper petals in the gutter

Flipping the Script

a cannon for the elegy
an elegy for the canon
a picnic for soft toys

friends in the Sunshine State
friends in California
poor postal you!

horizon line of wet trees over the roof
grey garden and forecasts of sleet
without prospect of purgatory or paradise

carrying a mirror to reflect colleagues
sit back and watch your money grow
a rain of frogs makes perfect sense

we've definitely flipped the script
learning in the end what the cost
and listening to the darkness, night

Hallucogenic Tourism

I hardly see the usual language.
Our current situation is the result
of these very words themselves!

One is entitled to take false steps,
they is the myth of the cultural
lighting ways to be elsewhere.

No chronicler could take his feather
without leaving for the flight of it;
but often he will not say it. Me,

I say it without voice opening out
because always in front of the eyes
there is nothing to occupy the spirit.

You speak about what I listen to,
seek to try include and understand.
It is precisely what one should not do,

we gains nothing. It is remarkable,
improvisation during this one hour
does not answer your any question.

Deposit hope of rationalization
along with understanding in the cloak
-room and let you grab the intuitive:

smell of washing powder in the alley,
along with passion flower. Cellophane
and newspaper, chipped thermos flask.

I Guess That's Why You Called it the Blues
for Robert Sheppard

   the night had a thousand 'i's

passionate threads of hidden living
offstage violence partially glimpsed

perverted by history's narratives
the table cluttered with opinion

   his 'i's were Pearl's

a further thread begins to reveal itself
it is not an abstract process

ventriloquism caulks and tightens bolts
offers media images of trouble

the first appearance of riot shields
somewhere within the dark study

protest always considered legitimate
she wants him more than anything

pleasure pulled from head of the shaft
language lays naked under glass vault lights

trimming rock with horizontal air drill
a fountain on the rooftop of the casino

Subway Shirt Hospital is some way off
along the bombed and firelit street

my 'i's adored you

defensive measure against the known
cut-and-cover sets a precedent

presence and precipitation
surveillance and subversion

lines of flight through language
parrot chatter in the grate

subsidence's excavated spoils
counterculture memories seized

whoever your readers and critics are
I hope the singing transmutes desire

emptiness takes my breath away
the inner voice finishes mid-sentence

the 'i's have it

to the amazement of everyone paying attention
work finished months before the deadline

a poem intrigued by colossal engineering
the face of the storefront shorn away

the petrifying talk of freedom
here taken literally

Its Own Journey

A dictaphone recording its own journey,
repeatedly sent to an invented address.
Each time it comes back: *Return to sender*.

Low level flights made under the radar,
journeys into silence and being alone
whilst you are away: faded postmarks,

sound of a door closing, the hiss of ancient tape.
Colour needing to be itself; trapped shadows
a mirage, however clear it sometimes seems.

Any fixed opinions I may have are challenged
by your letters and this sense of motion –
travel sickness brought on by staying at home.

I am alive to faint voices on the line,
strangers more *other* in their associations,
telling me what I should think and know.

Such instruction may not be inappropriate,
offers possible channels to be explored;
each word and phrase turned into a poem.

Just One of an Ongoing Series

Take pleasure in the world outside, then
when you can, despatch it somewhere else
There are so many places in the catalogue
more like home than home can ever be.

Notice each line has the same number of words
and enjoys paths that turn off into the unseen,
consider the properties of electrons,
the plastic backs of these borrowed chairs.

Staff shortages make for the predictable:
just one of an ongoing series of days
with particular focus on past events,
smoke coiled around tomorrow's ruins.

Excuse my disjunctivitis and eyewash –
I am inventing false memories of you.
Read with emotional, not literal, narrative,
I'm sure that history is not what it seems.

KING FOR A DAY

"I'm not one that folks hold on to. I ain't ever been prickly enough
to cling, nor yet smooth enough to grasp, which is the same as most folk.
I'm just a pebble that never got weathered through."
   —*The Jersey Shore*, William Mayne

Arguments with others,
multiple voices and stories,
the crackle of cellophane rain –
take note of these interruptions.

For this is the noise we make
as we reach out for tomorrow.
Oh, how hard we have to try
to navigate around the past.

I don't want to be heavy-handed
but can't help but be interested
in storms and discontinuities,
the glimmer of morning light.

There's plenty to be unhappy about
and little to show us the way –
only the twitch of imagination,
the glamour of forgotten songs.

I'm careful not to overdo allusion,
much too shy to make myself at home;
I admit my eye's not what it was,
agree it's not the weather's fault.

Notice I am using the present tense,
and ignoring the blood on the floor.
I like my world but I want it changed
now: a new city and skyline will do.

I spend my time looking out of the window,
prefer the word *sustain* rather than *survive*.
Keep a mind ready for the pastoral
and please curtsey or bow when you leave.

Magpie

random sample jukebox alarm
foregrounded word acquisition

born into language remembering
songs only the male birds sing

lightning flash destabilizing text
tone ghosting all the things we are

carnival folklore below the branches
when the going gets dark light the star

other true self multiple variations
we speak in each other's words

animating lists: the hat, the chair,
the smoke, the bones, the fact

a twilight coalition of the unwilling
story without end until the sun dies

a few incidents in the stillhouse
gold resonator night wearing feathers

MILK MONITOR
for Peter Blegvad

Your passion poured over the table
and started to curdle. Why did milk
consume you so? What made you care?

X pints in Y cartons, you said. *And cheese.
If you'd collected quotes for thirty-plus years
you'd know. Drunk in the places I've been . . .*

Your stories stunned us, the music
spoke as well. You didn't let up and
we didn't let you go. We wanted to

question, were hoping to know more.
If you could would you change the world?
I no longer believe that change is possible.

*I have learned to cultivate obsession.
Pick one from the list or select a new
abstraction, a source of irrational power.*

*There is a deep-seated need for miracles;
even the angels confuse milk and marble.
Absence can be a very strong prompt:*

a bird long since dead sings in our forest.

Neo-Shaman

inherited gesture
possible hesitation
surface appearance
question of degree

obligation

stumbling block
pause or hesitation
painting the painting
half the story

Quite the Adoring Hologram

I'll get to the rest of this stuff as & when,
the repeat prescriptions of landscape,
these grown-up catalogues of light.

Imagine the centre of strangeness,
the place where everything comes from;
progress lurches about all over the place.

There's more rumble here than decision:
vandalised interventions and forecasts
and ten times the available meaning.

Let angels steal the text and slip away.
Mind's a broken window, experience a trap;
everything points to endless dialogue.

Don't we need to look between times?
Between things? Our focus slips toward
pleasures to come. Thanks for sending

but count me out. The strange scent
of tomorrow is history. I recognise
how she walks, the angle of gravity.

I've known of miracles, but what's left
is a name engraved on the gallery wall:
your biography one last locked door.

Speed of Light

White dust and an uncanny stillness . . .
The mind's inclination to fabricate
more or less what we are, resides
inside our chosen boundary points.

Sometimes, fitful flashes of memory
sweep into a corner of the room;
all my friends, living and dead,
are outside, shouting in the street.

I'm only the caretaker of these words
and am not sure I've used them right.
They always seem to stack up wrong
then wobble before falling over.

I savour the moment gravity demands,
invent new strategies, make other plans.
Living is an exploratory gesture –
we try to make it all mean something.

Alert to the task concealed in this method,
I take pleasure in a world of false perspective
where nothing is required or expected to be true.
The journeys we can make span impossibility.

It's best not to know where you're going,
to seek anew the presence of the world;
self-erasure has been declared out of bounds,
but like all true gifts it cannot be refused.

If you trip over the wireless in the dark
you will hurt yourself and the music will stop;
if thought is exhausted then what we must do
is keep silent and move on, exploring the night.

Sunflower

'Everything is a guide,
I had thought
But then the world would be here
Only to keep us from becoming lost'
—'The New Season', James McCorkle

    apocalyptic end of things   final line conclusion
     scrambling how time works   learning how to fly
   constant failure to levitate   pushed into slow descent
      lurking in the shadows   tiny closet of a room
       real chemistry at work   radical translation
reincarnation of some sort   poems of my own making

   backwards through art history   sequences or series
       silent conversations   more coherent speech
      find out information   make up your own mind
     overhaul the alphabet   progress forward now
     artificial intelligence   an awful thing to say
 discover where we are going   luring people away

    carpeted from wall to wall   edited start to finish
 outrageous and high-handed   gonna walk all over you
forming its own structure   moving through the room
     hostile to performance   make the world my own
  brief instances of darkness   comets in the sky
     laws of love and pity   rockets to the moon

       diversity and access   contents of the mind
  misplaced sense of importance   emotionally attached
  exclamation-marked horizon   attempting to belong
   field trips and rock formations   articulate aloud
   exploring unlit passages   ambition's constant charm
weathered skylights black with age   spray painting in the dark

everything is mentioned   but there is no real proof
forgotten footnotes in the text   diverse community
    slight differences of detail   revolution's end
would have to be repeated   could not be otherwise
always illness or accident   inflicting harm by glance
    no taboo on looking   be silent do not touch

    familiar as wooden piers   splinters in every tree
expert in dramatic productions   sad and backward glance
elderflower tea and strawberry wine   chestnuts and walnuts too
    dynamite theologians   looking after spiritual needs
    after argument or visit   things begin to improve
    walk about the streets alone   centre of the world

grand corridors of power and glass   past is common to us all
    you get to play the hero then   write the final scene
    conjure up demons and wizards   beauty of water's song
    four minutes to cross the river   secret travel plans
chained to the gates of the palace   buried alive in a tomb
        no mourning or apology   death is terminal

hopscotch involves a pattern of squares   sent messages reach mum
    nobody must break the chain   keep quiet about the corpse
oak trees are safe in electric storms   belong to both and neither world
    the plumbing is in disarray   we nearly got washed away
    love comes from being vulnerable   a memory of popular songs
    rain on an empty playing field   water from out of the clouds

    individual sequences and poems   who and what I once was
    tomatoes ripening in autumn sun   not definitive, incomplete
    a question about interpretation   the reader co-creates
        making better choices   trying to find the time
    impatient and impetuous   not into end of line rhyme
    invasion as noble effort   corresponding with all my friends

japanese maple in autumn sun   moment in the mind
turn from the sleeping woman   she is not looking at me
scrutiny and interrogation   emerging from the self
sensuous level of perception   wild laugh of relief
face lit up softly sheds the years   emotions without cause
current theories of the mind   I am trying to get home

knots have long figured in magic   ties us all to the mast
strings and magnets and clockwork   like the back of my hand
we don't live near heaven   knowledge blinks out of view
question the nature of music   sound engulfs the room
low light leaking from metaphor   signal fading then gone
it is all there so to speak   faith structures defeating the eye

lots to interest and entertain   things we've all heard about
limited time high turnaround   repeated fractures and breaks
frequent loud interruptions   someone has something to say
start out with different intentions   in isolation now
at the centre of the story   said I looked like her son
long way to go for transcendence   my whole being shakes

mirror, inkblot, shadow, chair   puzzles of different shapes
two simple loops the very same size   drawings made out of names
complete or partial anagrams   a hundred empty rooms
rejection through the letterbox   interrupted plans
always intense and personal   a huge amount of work
names have a special significance   it's time to leave the stage

nothing less than everything   private self and public world
training as a visionary   cheap teenage punks with guns
medium of transformation   the touch of a dead man's hand
history requires that fear   made several attempts to speak
words lost through coastal erosion   rethinking the time
an occasion to see beyond this   nowhere in her eyes

over the hills and far away   music played till dawn
end of the world flickers into view   stretching from earth to sky
chronological familiarity   no time left to spare
overwhelming restlessness   destination made quite clear
structure is now cellular   a circle of events
closed eyes see the mirror   the magic morning is here

prayer flags strung out in the wind   mountains in the mist
the future stood around to view   moments undefined
repeated rites of passage   life cycles built for one
debris from exploded buddhas   caves in which to hide our souls
hummingbird returns to me   frozen in mid-air
summoning angels to quiz them   phrases older than rhyme

questions to be answered   dead husband in her dreams
apple and orange on three sticks   spring greenery and flowers
evil eye and borrowed pail   speak ill of absent friends
never struck by lightning   burnt with a blue flame
straw torches or small bonfires   what we have never seen
all things turn and spin and change   restlessness resumes

representation of temporal aspects   their morale was intact
someone will get it into their head   the intercom might have failed
down the lane past the houses   the sheer chaos that war brings
blear-eyed google and squinting   makes physical demands
draw the same line down the canvas   trample corn to pick the flowers
self-disgust and unvoiced rage   out of the house for hours

sunflower waiting to bud in September   a kind of refining move
specialisation producing restlessness   the next turn on the right
try and upset our way of seeing   digital photographs and film
doodles on small bits of paper   blown up very large
my office is a dining table   parent to all these words
fifteen squares in a dark tunnel   reports from another world

trying to write an alphabet with sand   in a busy rush-hour street
a city of the future   got everything it should
twisted circles make a chain   be sure that it's complete
writing an imaginary letter   words glued to a sign
hang a string across the room   photocopy the world outside
ask to be buried out of doors   where the dead and living join

unamity of opinion   only increases mystique
this thing could peel a planet   a crescendo of yells and leaps
slowly squeezed out of the picture   shabby symbols of life
large slabs of polished black granite   heads studying the floor
derangement of the senses   looking filthy and sad
further riots would follow   spearheading the new sound

versions of songs with similar tunes   another burnt-out old ruin
a kind of recuperation at work   this piece not conceptual at all
pointing hissing and stamping   next morning blind in one eye
real things were distant   reason a weathered stone
surprise blurred by vibration   everything in the shade
biting their thin bony knuckles   threshold of heaven and earth

we have known adjustment   illustrated tomes
collaborated together   working in various styles
often a good balance to be found   visions of magic and string
intelligence taste and feeling   known for disturbing the peace
hoping to receive an answer   hands and arms above the head
do not doubt in asking   futile gestures and signs

x marked on the treasure map   information is unique
people want us to have attitude   start unloading the van
invisible drawings in whiteness   we'll never work again
barely noticeable atmosphere   sound obscured and transformed
unbroken skin emits a high pitch   drowning in its own tune
prayer and liturgical activity   always looking down

yes the moon is full tonight   planning may take three years
open space is the best use of land   treasured and lucky ground
ecological concerns have been voiced   tidal marshes must be filled
leaves only when he chooses   stones in his or her hand
timber platform or extension   dangerous starlight and dreams
a call to prayer for the living   spirits gather as well

z what we use to symbolize snores   constant access to the noise
little stabs of happiness   smiles reflected in other's frowns
retire and live in lofty seclusion   two feet dragging slow
surface rather than chamber   unmuscled as a child
a recording of past and specific place   neither human nor machine
a far away hum of voices   beautiful as last night's dream

Treading Some Well-Worn Tracks

Intrigued by sequences and projects as published,
I test tube the world and falsify writing in the desert.
Love transcends revelation and challenge;
the majority of poetry bores me. Individual poets' work
excites but is so often just ferret emptiness.

Revelation uses alphabetical or other structural devices,
prose poems with fraudulent habitats and wildlife,
test-tube culture and socio-politics. Fear is becoming
the fastest growing experience in the shock of the world;
a kind of framing device in the book of interviews I reviewed.

Send us peace and turmoil, bumps and irregularities,
a life supply of spirit. List all bizarre poems that are witty
and light up the dark, stop writing for quite a while,
try to allow paper for all. Get used to new ways and things
that can't work; readers aren't stupid unless they choose to be.

Freeriding gives associative deserts, offering
several intelligent ways to paddle through words
if an author is finding it difficult, a famous writing journey:
the wasteland versus inspiration, ostrich tossed in time,
with selected poems as a physical accomplishment.

I turn to the deep possibilities opened up. Poetry
doesn't have arctic expanses, tell stories or say anything,
it can be playful, arranged visually, can try and reproduce
the fastest growing way we think and challenge. Now
I have wildlife, wasteland, space open and seemingly casual.

Poetry should infuriate, bemuse, annoy and puzzle, help
construct a place. I calculate habitats and conversations
with the mind, a sponge originally designed by NASA.
Space is a physical, spiritual oasis the reader can dance in;
its very promise a spiritual global positioning device.

Wild Root

Our problems end with peculiar friendship.
All we have is a diagram for making,
yet the construction of tidiness eludes me.

Sleep and dreams are discarded each morning
rolled up and tied neatly with garden string,
put out for the birds to peck and take away.

Shells, beads and small dolls must be left
as arranged; things will then be perfect.
I go looking for order after forgetting

where I left whatever I am looking for.
I had a red bicycle for getting back home
but somebody stole it and rode it away.

A woman leaps from a tower, the suspect's hair
was found mixed up with the victim's clothes.
Everyone is guilty when the curtain falls.

Sources

'White-Out': letter from Peter Dent; Alistair Fitchett's blog | 'A More Personal Invention': *An Anthology of New Poetics*, ed. Christopher Beach | 'The Lights are on at this Point': letter from Jay Ramsay | 'Winging It': letter from Peter Dent; Clement Greenber, quoted in *Modern Painters* vol 14 no 4; Mario Merz sculpture title, CAIXA Foundation, Barcelona | 'On the Horizon': *Kingdom of the Edge*, Jay Ramsay; *Rocking the Classics*, Edward Macan; *zeros + ones*, Sadie Plant | 'A Beautiful Wind': poems by Peter Dent; *Jorie Graham. Essays on the Poetry*, ed. Thomas Gardner; 'His Words', David Grubb | 'Thunder at the David Lynch Hotel': *Artaud: The Screaming Body*, Stephen Barber; *Horse Latitudes*, Jay Merrick | 'Nyctalopia': letter from Peter Dent; *Problem Pictures*, Spencer Selby; *China*, Alan Wall | 'Endlessly Divisible': *Tapies. The Complete Works*, Anna Agustí; *Little Green Man*, Simon Armitage; *Justified Sinners*, eds. Ross Birrell & Alec Finlay; *Contexts of Poetry*, Robert Creeley; letter from Peter Dent; *Richard Diebenkorn. Ocean Park*, Jack Flam; Anthony Key catalogue; *Slowly*, Lyn Hejinian; *Kind of Blue*, Ashley Kahn; *The Turbulent Term of Tyke Tiler*, Gene Kemp; 'The Haunting', David Kennedy; *The President of Earth*, David Kennedy; *Knowledge* magazine; Jo Milne catalogue; *Modern Painters*, Autumn 2002; *Sputnik Sweetheart*, Haruki Murakami; *Secularisation*, Edward Norman; email from Jane Routh; *The Street of Crocodiles*, Bruni Schulz; *William Scott. Paintings and Drawings* [catalogue]; *London Orbital*, Iain Sinclair; *About Religion*, Mark C. Taylor; *Ocean of Sound*, David Toop; Chuang Tzu; *Reading Series Fiction*, Victor Watson; *Wide Closed Spaces* anthology | 'The Uncertain Future': *Industrial* Poetics, Joe Amato; *Writing the Bright Moment*, ed. Roselle Angwin; *Illumine. Garry Fabian Miller*, Martin Barnes; *Digital Leatherette*, Steve Beard; *Meat Puppet Alphabet*, Steve Beard; *The Conspiracy of Art*, Jean Baudrillard; *Writing Space*, Jay David Bolter; *Four British Fantasists*, Charles Butler; *The Court of Good Intentions*, Michael Byers; *Peter Lanyon. Modernism and the Land*, Andrew Causey; *Instant Light. Tarkovsky Polaroids*, eds. Giovanni Chiaramonte and Andrew A. Tarkovsky; 'Beat Godfather Meets Glitter Mainman', Craig Copetas; *Love Songs*, Crass; letters and poems from Peter Dent; 'Tony Cragg, the Poetics of the Fragment and Proportion'. Danilo Eccher; *Parables of Disfiguration*, Robert Eisenhauer; *Da Capo Best Music Writing 2006*, ed. Mary Gaitskill' *Jorie Graham. Essays on the Poetry*, ed. Thomas Gardner; *The Dominion of the Dead*, Robert Pogue Harrison; *Confusion Incorporated*, Stewart Home; *Independent on Sunday*, 19.11.06; *Literature & the Urban Experience*, eds. Michael C Jay and Ann Chalmers Watts; *What Is Poetry*, Daniel Kane; *Blade Runner*, Nick Lacey; *Meaning Performance*, Tony Lopez; letter from Ray Malone; *Voice of the Fire*, Alan Moore; *New Media Poetics*, eds. Adelaide Morris and Thomas Swiss; NAWE conference, Brunel University, November 2006; *Wising Up the Marks. The Amodern William Burroughs*, Timothy S. Murphy; *Sentence #4*; *The Trouble with Genius*, Bob Perelman; *Real Cities*, Steve Pile; *Retaking the Universe*, eds. Davis Schneiderman & Philip Walsh; *Connected*, Steven Shapiro; *Fashionable Noise: on Digital* Poetics,

Brian Kim Stefans; *Imagologies. Media Philosophy*, Mark C. Taylor & Esa Saarinen; David Smith, Karen Wilkin; *The Best American Spiritual Writing 2006*, ed. Philip Zaleski | 'The Uncertain Future': *Industrial* Poetics, Joe Amato; *Writing the Bright Moment*, ed. Roselle Angwin; *Illumine. Garry Fabian Miller*, Martin Barnes; *Digital Leatherette*, Steve Beard; *Meat Puppet Alphabet*, Steve Beard; *The Conspiracy of Art*, Jean Baudrillard; *Writing Space*, Jay David Bolter; *Four British Fantasists*, Charles Butler; *The Court of Good Intentions*, Michael Byers; *Peter Lanyon. Modernism and the Land*, Andrew Causey; *Instant Light. Tarkovsky Polaroids*, eds. Giovanni Chiaramonte and Andrew A. Tarkovsky; 'Beat Godfather Meets Glitter Mainman', Craig Copetas; *Love Songs*, Crass; letters and poems from Peter Dent; 'Tony Cragg, the Poetics of the Fragment and Proportion'. Danilo Eccher; *Parables of Disfiguration*, Robert Eisenhauer; *Da Capo Best Music Writing 2006*, ed. Mary Gaitskill; *Jorie Graham. Essays on the Poetry*, ed. Thomas Gardner; *The Dominion of the Dead*, Robert Pogue Harrison; *Confusion Incorporated*, Stewart Home; *Independent on Sunday*, 19.11.06; *Literature & the Urban Experience*, eds. Michael C Jay and Ann Chalmers Watts; *What Is Poetry*, Daniel Kane; *Blade Runner*, Nick Lacey; *Meaning Performance*, Tony Lopez; letter from Ray Malone; *Voice of the Fire*, Alan Moore; *New Media Poetics*, eds. Adelaide Morris and Thomas Swiss; NAWE conference, Brunel University, November 2006; *Wising Up the Marks. The Amodern William Burroughs*, Timothy S. Murphy; *Sentence #4*; *The Trouble with Genius*, Bob Perelman; *Real Cities*, Steve Pile; *Retaking the Univere*, seds. Davis Schneiderman & Philip Walsh; *Connected*, Steven Shapiro; *Fashionable Noise: on Digital* Poetics, Brian Kim Stefans; *Imagologies. Media Philosophy*, Mark C. Taylor & Esa Saarinen; David Smith, Karen Wilkin; *The Best American Spiritual Writing 2006*, ed. Philip Zaleski | 'Crease Patterns': *Drafts*, Rachel Blau DuPlessis; 'The Serial as Portal': an interview with Rachel Blau DuPlessis, Chris McCreary; http://www.paperfolding.com/history/; http://www.sarahsorigami.com/"; http://www.kid-at-art.com; http://www.ulster.net/~spider/origami.htm | 'Jazz Heart Electric': 'Trust me, I'm a rock star', Tom Cox; 'Serene Team', Ekow Eshun; 'Poetry City', Cole Swensen | 'A Fire in the House of Ice': *American Poetry Review*, July/August 2006, vol. 35/No.4; 'Working Notes', Andrew Benjamin, in *Basilisk 2*, http://www.basilisk.com; *Bomb*, Summer 2006, no. 96; email from Andy Brown; 'Sphere of influence – Passages – Mario Merz – Biography', Germano Celant, in *Artforum* 2004; *Theories of Modern Art*, ed. Herschel B. Chipp; 'To Get Us Thinking', Ian Cowan, in *Quadrant*, May 2004, vol. XLVIII no.5; letter from Peter Dent; *Full Spectrum* catalogue; *Jorie Graham. Essays on the Poetry*, ed. Thomas Gardner; *High Lonesome*, ed. Adam Giannelli; 'Mario Merz's Language', Giorgio Guglielmino, in *Mario Merz*, Fundación Proa catalogue 2003; *Chroma*, Derek Jarman; *Make Poetry History*, Luke Kennard & Rupert Loydell; *Edwina Leapman. Thirty Years at Annely Juda Fine Art*; *Meaning Performance*, Tony Lopez; 'Pre-Fab View', in *Ex Catalogue*, Rupert M Loydell; *Mario Merz*, Galleria Civica d'Arte Contemporanea, Tranto; *Ian Stephenson. And our eyes scan Time.*; *Television*, Jean-Phillipe Toussaint; *Mario Merz*, hopefulmonster 1995; *Mario Merz*, Fundación Proa 2003; *Mario Merz*, hopefulmonster 2003; *Mario Merz.Domenico Bianchi*, Bari,

Castello Svevo catalogue 2004; 'Mario Merz's Future of an Illusion', Jeanne Silverthorne; http://www.speronewestwater.com; 'Mario Merz Works Complement the Guggenheim', Roberta Smith, in *New York Times*, Sept 29 1989; 'The formal in art and its acceptance', Jan van de Pavert; *The Jimi Hendrix Companion*, ed. Chris Potash; The *Modern Poetic Sequence*, M.L. Rosenthal & Sally M. Gall; http://ronsilliman.blogspot.com, Saturday, November 15, 2003; http://www.sfu.ca/archaeology/museum/danielle_longhouse/keepers/housing.html | 'At Home': letter from Peter Dent | 'Consider this My Accidental Suicide Note': *Black Clock* #6 | 'Counterfeit Word Jar': *bagne, or Criteria for Heaven*, rob mclennan; *The Spirit of Prague*, Ivan Klíma; 'everything will be coded>>>isolation' a list by Sunset Killer, amazon.co.uk | 'Cross-Purposes': letter from Peter Dent; *Napoli's Walls*, Louis Sclavis; *Don't Ask Me What I Mean*, eds. Clare Brown and Don Paterson | Dedicated to Compulsion': *Black Clock* #6 | 'Discontinuity': *American Poetry Review* vol. 32, no.4; *Girl in a Garden*, Lesley Chamberlain; letters and poems from Peter Dent; Bill Nelson, *Hex* website; *American Women Poets in the 21st Century*, eds. Claudia Rankine and Juliana Spahr; *Arcana*, ed. John Zorn; *Removed for Further Study, The Gig 13/14*; *Tears in the Fence* no. 35 | 'Entangled': *Entanglement*, Allen Fisher; *The Boy who Taught the Beekeeper to Read*, Susan Hill; *A Nomad Poetics*, Pierre Joris | 'Flipping the Script': letter from Peter Dent; *a matrix of meanings*, Craig Detweiler & Barry Taylor | 'I Guess that's Why You Called it The Blues': *Violent London*, Clive Bloom; *A Nomad Poetics*, Pierre Joris; *The City Beneath Us*, New York Transit Museum; *Tin Pan Arcadia*, Robert Sheppard; email from Robert Sheppard | 'Its Own Journey': letters from Peter Dent and Neil Roberts | 'Just One of an Ongoing Series': letter from Peter Dent; *An Exeter Mis-Guide*, Wrights & Sites; *Poetry Salzburg Review* no. 5 | 'King for a Day': *American Poetry Review* vol. 32, no.4; letters and poems from Peter Dent; Bill Nelson, *Hex* website; *Arcana*, ed. John Zorn; *Removed for Further Study, The Gig 13/14* | 'Magpie': *Signal to Noise* #46, summer 2006; 'Plunderverse: A Cartographic Manifesto', Gregory Betts | Neo-Shaman': *Jason Martin*, Andrew Denton | 'Quite the Adoriong Hologram': poems and letter from Peter Dent | 'Speed of Light': *Girl in a Garden*, Lesley Chamberlain; *American Women Poets in the 21st Century*, eds. Claudia Rankine and Juliana Spahr; *An Exeter Mis-Guide*, Wrights & Sites; *Removed for Further Study, The Gig 13/14* | 'Treading Some Well-Worn Tracks': *bagne, or Criteria for Heaven*, rob mclennan; *The Spirit of Prague*, Ivan Klíma; 'everything will be coded>>>isolation' a list by Sunset Killer, amazon.co.uk; *Vallum* submission guidelines | 'Wild Root': *Don't Ask Me What I Mean*, eds. Clare Brown and Don Paterson.

www.ingramcontent.com/pod-product-compliance
Lightning Source LLC
Chambersburg PA
CBHW022011160426
43197CB00007B/390